ARISTOT
A GUIDE FOR THE

Guides for the Perplexed

Continuum's *Guides for the Perplexed* are clear, concise and accessible introductions to thinkers, writers and subjects that students and readers can find especially challenging. Concentrating specifically on what it is that makes the subject difficult to grasp, these books explain and explore key themes and ideas, guiding the reader towards a thorough understanding of demanding material.

Guides for the Perplexed available from Continuum:

Adorno: A Guide for the Perplexed, Alex Thomson
Deleuze: A Guide for the Perplexed, Claire Colebrook
Derrida: A Guide for the Perplexed, Julian Wolfreys
Descartes: A Guide for the Perplexed, Justin Skirry
Existentialism: A Guide for the Perplexed, Stephen Earnshaw
Freud: A Guide for the Perplexed, Celine Surprenant
Gadamer: A Guide for the Perplexed, Chris Lawn
Habermas: A Guide for the Perplexed, Eduardo Mendieta
Hegel: A Guide for the Perplexed, David James
Hobbes: A Guide for the Perplexed, Stephen J. Finn
Hume: A Guide for the Perplexed, Angela Coventry
Husserl: A Guide for the Perplexed, Matheson Russell
Kant: A Guide for the Perplexed, TK Seung
Kierkegaard: A Guide for the Perplexed, Clare Carlisle
Levinas: A Guide for the Perplexed, B.C. Hutchens
Leibniz: A Guide for the Perplexed, Franklin Perkins
Merleau-Ponty: A Guide for the Perplexed, Eric Matthews
Nietzsche: A Guide for the Perplexed, R. Kevin Hill
Plato: A Guide for the Perplexed, Gerald A. Press
Quine: A Guide for the Perplexed, Gary Kemp
Ricoeur: A Guide for the Perplexed, David Pellauer
Rousseau: A Guide for the Perplexed, Matthew Simpson
Sartre: A Guide for the Perplexed, Gary Cox
Spinoza: A Guide for the Perplexed, Charles Jarrett
Wittgenstein: A Guide for the Perplexed, Mark Addis

ARISTOTLE: A GUIDE FOR THE PERPLEXED

JOHN A. VELLA

continuum

Continuum International Publishing Group

The Tower Building
11 York Road
London
SE1 7NX

80 Maiden Lane
Suite 704
New York
NY 10038

www.continuumbooks.com

First published 2008

British Library Cataloguing-in-Publication Data
A catalogue record for this book is available from the British Library.

ISBN-10: HB: 0-8264-9707-1
PB: 0-8264-9708-X
ISBN-13: HB: 978-0-8264-9707-9
PB: 978-0-8264-9708-6

British Library Cataloguing-in-Publication Data
A catalogue record for this book is available from the British Library.

Library of Congress Cataloging-in-Publication Data
A catalog record for this book is available from the Library of Congress.

Typeset by Servis Filmsetting Ltd, Manchester
Printed and bound in Great Britain by
MPG Books Ltd, Bodmin, Cornwall

For my wife Amelia with all my love

CONTENTS

CONTENTS

ACKNOWLEDGEMENTS

My greatest debt is to those teachers from whom I have learned so much about Aristotle. Professor Grace Ledbetter at Swarthmore College and Professor Georgios Anagnostopoulos at the University of California at San Diego have both been invaluable as teachers of Ancient Philosophy generally and Aristotle in particular. I am also indebted to Greg Shirley and Matt Egan for reading earlier drafts and making helpful suggestions. Any errors that remain are of course my own. I would also like to thank the editorial staff at Continuum Publishing; Sarah Douglas, Tom Crick and Adam Green have all provided assistance from the earliest to the final stages of this project.

I am also grateful to Princeton University Press for permission to quote from the Revised Oxford Translation of the following texts: *Metaphysics*, *Physics*, *On the Soul* and *Nicomachean Ethics*, all found in J. Barnes, *The Complete Works of Aristotle*. Ó (1984, The Jowett Copyright Trustees). Reprinted by permission of Princeton University Press.

CHRONOLOGY

INTRODUCTION

In his fourteenth-century masterpiece *The Divine Comedy*, Dante
Alighieri created the most famous and enduring literary image of
Aristotle. As the poet Virgil guides Dante's pilgrim, the two come
upon a scene in the first circle of hell, often referred to as Limbo.
Our pilgrim describes seeing numerous figures from the ancient
world. Here is his account of seeing the philosophers and scientists
of antiquity:

> I raised my eyes a little, and there he was,
> Who is called Master of those who know,
> Sitting in a philosophic family
> Who look upon him and do him honour.
> I saw nearest to him Plato and Socrates. (*Inferno*, Canto IV.130–5)[1]

Our pilgrim continues by naming the individuals who surround the
Master in this philosophic family. The only person who is not named
is the one who does not need to be named. Everyone in Dante's
world knew exactly to whom the pilgrim referred. Only one man
could be called *Master of those who know* and *The Philosopher*. That
man is of course Aristotle.

There are a few points I would like to highlight regarding this
remarkable image. First, we can note that Dante's pilgrim has to
raise his eyes to gaze upon Aristotle and his philosophical
family. Though the pilgrim's journey through hell involves endless
descents, that pattern is broken in the case of Aristotle. Even in
hell, one must look up to see Aristotle; even in hell, Aristotle is at
the summit. We can also note that the historical order of these
philosophers of antiquity is inverted in this image. Socrates was a

teacher of Plato, and Plato was a teacher of Aristotle; in Dante's vision, the last pupil in this historical sequence represents the highest achievement among these men. In life, Aristotle studied under Plato; in the afterlife, Plato, Socrates and indeed all learned men look to Aristotle and pay him homage. Dante's scene thus suggests extraordinary admiration for Aristotle; we almost forget that Aristotle and his philosophic family are in the outermost circle of hell. While much of the *Inferno* is filled with what Jeffers has called Dante's 'dirty / Political hatreds', this scene is exceptional for its compassion and respect for Aristotle and the philosophers of antiquity.[2]

There is no mystery as to why Dante held Aristotle in high esteem. No human being before or since has towered over human wisdom as Aristotle did. From his death in 322 BC until the rediscovery of Plato's works during the Renaissance, Aristotle reigned supreme and unchallenged as the master of those who know. Aristotle's intellectual range is absolutely astonishing; he wrote in every field of human inquiry, and he was considered the ultimate authority in nearly every subject. Centuries of philosophical and scientific scholarship focused entirely on expounding and interpreting the writings of Aristotle. It is difficult for us to fathom Aristotle's intellectual stature and influence. We live in a highly specialized age in which even the most intellectually ambitious among us can only hope to master our specialty. A survey of the geniuses of our age confirms this trend toward specialization: consider Einstein's mastery of physics or Freud's understanding of the human psyche. Rare is the individual who makes significant contributions to more than one field; rarest of all is the individual who makes defining contributions to every field. Such a man was Aristotle. To be sure, Aristotle mastered human knowledge and inquiry at a time when both were still in their infancy. Nevertheless, his achievements defined the known world for nearly two millennia.

Aristotle's stature and influence today are not due to his mastery of facts or theories. Much of what he took to be facts has been disproved; most of his theories are now widely regarded as false. Rather, Aristotle is a giant of philosophy and science because of the awesome power of his *method*. Aristotle was utterly relentless in his pursuit of knowledge; his life was ruled by an overwhelming desire to know. In his pursuit of knowledge, he developed a powerful and fertile method of analysis that is part of the very fabric of all subsequent philosophical and scientific thought. Aristotle bequeathed to us a rich conceptual apparatus through which we can continue his inquiries. Thus as we read Aristotle we should be concerned not only with the doctrines that he seems to endorse; we should also attend to the questions he asks and the methods by which he attempts answers to those questions. Even though many of Aristotle's theories have been proven false, his method endures.

I here wish to highlight a key point about Aristotle's philosophical and scientific method. Aristotle is guided in his inquiries by a common-sense empiricism. For Aristotle, the stated goal of scientific explanation is to 'save the phenomena'. The phenomena are the appearances that we experience; the phenomena are the way things seem to our senses. It may sound uncontroversial to seek to save the phenomena, but Aristotle's approach is quite radical when compared with the rationalist tradition in Greek philosophy. Whereas other philosophers, notably Socrates, Plato and Parmenides, often explained away the phenomena or appearances as being unreal or false, Aristotle seeks to preserve the appearances and to explain how and why the appearances are the way they are. Aristotle's philosophy is thus guided by the intuition that our experiences of the world are largely true; thus our investigations of the world should begin with our investigations of the phenomena or appearances. This intuition is directly opposed to the rationalist intuition that the world of the senses is largely false, while reason reveals the real and true nature of things. Socrates, Plato and Parmenides all discredited appearances and insisted that we rely on reason alone to understand the world. If reason suggests something contrary to the appearances, then it is reason that should be trusted. Plato and Parmenides argue that the world is actually quite different from the way it seems to us.

Aristotle, however, claims that the world *is* largely as it *appears* to us. The philosophy and science that emerge from these competing intuitions are quite different. The rationalist tradition focuses on the intelligible rather than the sensible realm. For the rationalists, philosophy and science are primarily mathematical in form. These early rationalists even call into question the possibility of natural science. Aristotle is generally unimpressed by rational explanations unless they can save the phenomena. While the rationalists discredit natural science, for Aristotle natural science is a core part of the philosophical and scientific enterprise. This is not to suggest that Aristotle completely dismisses the rationalist tradition; to the contrary, he draws on that tradition and makes use of it where appropriate. But for Aristotle, reason must be relied upon to explain the appearances, not to explain away the appearances as unreal or false. The rationalist and empiricist intuitions reflect fundamentally different orientations towards the world. These orientations form the foundation for each philosopher's outlook on the world. For the rationalist, we begin with reason and follow it wherever it leads. For the empiricist, we begin with the phenomena and we employ reason to explain and save the phenomena.

THE LIFE OF ARISTOTLE

Aristotle was born in 384 BC in Stagira, a small town in northern Greece. His father, Nicomachus, was a physician; it is possible that the young Aristotle's interest in biology and anatomy began during his early acquaintance with his father's work. At age 17, Aristotle migrated to Athens to join Plato's Academy. The Academy offered the finest education in all of Greece, and Plato held the young Aristotle in high favour. The primary intellectual influence in Aristotle's life was Plato's philosophy. Aristotle was an excellent pupil, and his keen mind was already developing forceful criticisms of Plato's philosophy. Aristotle also made significant contributions to the Academy as a scholar. Many Platonists confined their inquiries to mathematics and geometry; Aristotle brought the pursuit of natural science to the Academy.

Upon the death of Plato in 347 BC, Aristotle left Athens and settled in Assos. His reasons for leaving Athens are not entirely clear. It has been suggested that the stewardship of the Academy after Plato represented to Aristotle the worst tendencies of Platonism; the Academy became more mathematical in its approach to philosophy. It is also likely that the changing political climate in Athens spurred Aristotle to leave. Though he was Greek, Aristotle was not an Athenian by birth. His father had connections to Macedon, and a rising tide of anti-Macedonian sentiment in Athens may have made life there uncomfortable for Aristotle. In Assos and later in Lesbos, Aristotle surrounded himself with learned individuals; he also undertook the greater portion of his biological inquiries during this time. He wrote extensively on natural history and the anatomy of animals.

In 343 BC, Aristotle's connections to Macedon resulted in an invitation from Philip of Macedon to tutor the young Alexander, then 13 years old. Aristotle accepted the invitation and the tremendous responsibility of educating a future ruler. Very little is known about the course of study in which Aristotle instructed his young pupil. There are suggestions of an intense romance between teacher and pupil, and also suggestions of considerable disagreements. Aristotle counselled against young Alexander's focus on action and imperial conquest. Aristotle's tutelage of Alexander ended in 340 BC when Alexander was appointed regent for his father. Aristotle likely settled in his hometown of Stagira until he returned to Athens in 335 BC.

Aristotle's return to Athens marks the beginning of the most fruitful period of his intellectual life. Just outside of Athens, Aristotle founded his own school, called the Lyceum. The Lyceum catered to both scholars and the general public. In the mornings, the Lyceum offered lectures on specialized and profound questions of philosophy and science. In the afternoons, there were lectures that appealed to a wider audience. Aristotle was not the only person who lectured at the Lyceum, but as the school's founder, he was the most accomplished lecturer. He also devoted himself to establishing a library at the Lyceum; hundreds of manuscripts were collected, and this library became the model for future great libraries. Aristotle contributed an enormous quantity of his own writings to this collection. It is generally agreed among scholars that most of Aristotle's extant works are from this period of 12 or 13 years during his leadership of the Lyceum. During this time he laid out the broad outlines of scientific inquiry, and he advanced many sciences beyond the points that had previously been attained.

When Aristotle's former pupil Alexander died in 323 BC, Aristotle's position in Athens again became untenable. Alexander had conquered the known world, though many of the Greek city-states bristled at being subsumed under Alexander's Greek Empire. Athens had always been a fiercely independent city-state, and upon Alexander's death another rising tide of anti-Macedonian sentiment overtook Athens. Aristotle's Macedonian connections again aroused the suspicions of the Athenians, and Aristotle was soon charged with impiety. Impiety was the precise charge upon which Socrates was convicted and sentenced to execution in 399 BC. Socrates was an Athenian, and if he could draw the ire of the Athenians, Aristotle seems to have felt that he as an outsider could not remain in Athens. Claiming that he would not allow Athens to commit a second crime against philosophy, Aristotle left Athens for Chalcis, where he died in 322 BC.

Such was the course of Aristotle's intellectual and public life. It is remarkable that a man devoted to intellectual pursuits felt twice compelled to leave the intellectual centre of Greece. As for Aristotle's private life, we know little. His will is often cited as evidence of his care and affection for others.[3] In his will, he made careful and generous provisions for his relatives and for his slaves. He ensured that his common-law wife and his teenage children would be cared for in a manner befitting a family of their status. His will guarded against his slaves being sold, and his will also arranged for the emancipation of several of his slaves. These are certainly indications of a gentle and caring nature. Aristotle lived too long ago for us to truly know what he was like as a person. From surviving documents, we are able to conclude that he was thoughtful and considerate, and that his life was ruled by a desire to know and inquire. Beyond this, it is difficult to reach any sure conclusions regarding the character of this extraordinary man.

THE WORKS OF ARISTOTLE

Of Aristotle's vast and diverse literary works, only about a fifth has survived. Even though most of his life's works are lost to us, we are still able to develop a fair idea of Aristotle's literary activities. The first point to note about the extant works of Aristotle is that most of them were never intended to be read or published. Scholars are now generally agreed that what has survived are most likely Aristotle's own lecture notes. Many of these are writings that he composed and edited over a number of years. These notes seem to be primarily for his use rather than for a reading public. In addition, though we read books of Aristotle as continuous treatises, he did not write them in this way. This is true of many of Aristotle's most famous works. For example, he did not organize his logical writings under the single heading of the *Organon*. Later editors did this. The *Metaphysics* is a collection of 14 different treatises arranged by a later editor under a single heading; we do not know if Aristotle would have consented to this editorial choice. The *Nicomachean Ethics* is a collection of Aristotle's ethical writings under a single title, perhaps arranged by one of Aristotle's sons. This helps to explain why many of Aristotle's works jump from one topic to another without explanation or transition; later editors tried to group his writings according to topics, but we have no way of knowing how Aristotle wanted his works to be presented.

These points about Aristotle's writings have a profound effect on our experience of reading Aristotle. Many people come to Aristotle's writings after reading Plato's dialogues, and they are often confused by Aristotle's style. The comparison with Plato is not fair to Aristotle. The difference between reading finished works and unfinished notes is immense. Plato's dialogues are finished works that were intended for publication and a reading audience. What is more, in Plato we have perhaps the finest writer in all of philosophy. Plato made it easy and enjoyable for us to read him; the philosophy is difficult, to be sure, but the literary form and style offer unparalleled joys. To read Aristotle, we must do some work and change our expectations.

One of the best ways to read Aristotle is to imagine yourself in the context of a lecture. Consider the different experiences of listening to a lecture and of giving a lecture. Reading Aristotle sometimes demands that you put yourself in each of these positions. It is sometimes helpful to imagine that you had to lecture from Aristotle's writings.[4] There are gaps and transitions that may need to be filled in; there are arguments and examples that may need elaboration and explanation. Some material may be central and require emphasis; other material may be treated as an aside or a tangent. A lecture is also more fluid than a finished treatise. Points of emphasis and the order of presentation can be varied. Lecturers can experiment with their raw material.

It can also be helpful to imagine that one is hearing a lecture as one reads Aristotle. Hearing a lecture is a very different experience, with different expectations, from reading a finished work. One cannot hope to grasp everything that one hears in a lecture; some points may require further research and reading; other points may leap out at you as being of vital importance. Ultimately the goal of a lecture is not to persuade the audience of a particular view, but rather to educate the audience on a subject and to inspire the audience to pursue the matter further. In this respect, Aristotle's writings are a resounding success.

Nearly every reader will find a passage or two on almost every page that spurs him or her to further study. Reading Aristotle sometimes feels like the whole world of learning and inquiry is opening up before you. You may not reach a sure conclusion reading Aristotle, but you will have a thorough sense for the intellectual terrain he discusses. Aristotle's writings invite us to join him in his pursuit of knowledge; his enthusiasm for learning is infectious. Aristotle is not just a great knower; he is a great teacher.

This book treats a selection of Aristotle's writings that are fundamental to his philosophical and scientific enterprise. This book is structured around five concepts that are basic to Aristotle, and hence, to the rest of philosophy: science, substance, nature, soul, and human flourishing. The first chapter treats Aristotle's notion of science (*episteme*); in the *Posterior Analytics*, Aristotle develops an account of the nature of scientific knowledge. The remaining four chapters treat specific sciences that conform in their structure and character to the vision of science laid out in the *Posterior Analytics*. Our second concept is substance or being (*ousia*); this concept is treated in Aristotle's *Metaphysics* and in the *Categories*. Before we can read anything else in the Aristotelian corpus, we must grapple with his treatment of substance. The science of substance, i.e. first philosophy or metaphysics, informs all other scientific endeavours. Our third concept is nature (*phusis*). Aristotle was an accomplished natural scientist, and in the *Physics* he lays out his views regarding nature and the science of nature. Our fourth concept is life or soul (*psuche*). For Aristotle, the most important distinction in the natural world is between that which lives and that which does not. He investigates that most wondrous of all natural phenomena – life – in his work *On the Soul*. Finally, after we progress through the preceding concepts, we are in a position to explore the science of human happiness or flourishing. This is the heart of Aristotle's ethics as developed in the *Nicomachean Ethics*. This is perhaps the richest of all of Aristotle's contributions to philosophy. These five concepts – science, substance, nature, soul, and human flourishing – will anchor our study of Aristotle.

These five concepts are not arcane or highly specialized subjects. Rather, they are subjects that should prove interesting and accessible to general readers of philosophy, history and science. Everyone has something to learn from Aristotle. Everyone can learn to think more clearly about any subject by reading Aristotle and engaging with his arguments. Anyone who wishes to learn more can surely benefit from an encounter with the man who desired to learn perhaps more than any other human being. Aristotle is often spoken of, sometimes derisively, as a common-sense philosopher. Aristotle is not a common-sense philosopher in the respect that his views are facile or merely popular. Rather, his philosophy is common sense in that it treats issues that are common to all human wondering and curiosity. Aristotle has the skills of a specialist, to be sure, but his motivation arises from a universal human curiosity. We can never hope to achieve what Aristotle accomplished in scholarship, but we can be encouraged by the fact that however great his achievements, he was like the rest of us in that he wondered about the world in which he lived.

We thus embark upon a most magnificent journey, guided by one of the greatest intellectual giants humanity has ever produced. This book is intended as a companion to Aristotle's writings. As such, I recommend the following editions of Aristotle's works, all of which are included in the bibliography. Ackrill has edited a compact edition of Aristotle's works in *A New Aristotle Reader*, published by Princeton University Press. McKeon has edited a more expansive collection entitled *The Basic Works of Aristotle*, published by Modern Library. Finally, Irwin and Fine have edited a collection entitled *Aristotle: Selections*, published by Hackett. Each of these collections is well organized and includes excellent translations. All of the works discussed in this book are included in each of these editions of Aristotle's works. If you suspect you may begin a lifelong affair with Aristotle's writings, you may wish to invest in *The Complete Works of Aristotle*, edited by Barnes and published by Princeton University Press. The point here is that one cannot understand Aristotle only through second-hand accounts; there is simply no substitute for reading Aristotle. The goal of this book is to help you develop the skills to read Aristotle on your own. In order for Aristotle to open up the known world for you, it is sometimes necessary to have help in opening up the world of Aristotle. It is my hope that this book provides its readers with direct access to the unrivalled works of Aristotle.

Aristotle's works are cited using the Bekker pages from the 1831 edition prepared by Immanuel Bekker. The Bekker pages are cited according to the following code: page number, column and line. Hence 1055a6–12 refers to Bekker page 1055, column a, lines 6–12.

These pages are printed in the margins of every scholarly edition of Aristotle's works, and this is the standard way of referring to Aristotle's works. Whatever edition of Aristotle's works you settle on, be sure that the Bekker pages are printed in the margins.

CHAPTER 1

SCIENCE (*EPISTEME*)

DIVISION OF THE SCIENCES ACCORDING TO AIMS AND OBJECTS

We begin by orienting ourselves with respect to the vast body of human knowledge. As we noted in the introduction, Aristotle wrote on every area of human inquiry, so if we attempt to trace Aristotle's various scientific investigations, we shall surely be overwhelmed. We shall find ourselves studying diverse and seemingly unconnected phenomena. But for Aristotle, as for Plato before him, science is not a random or haphazard amassing of facts. Rather, science is structured in a specific and logical way; scientific knowledge is structured according to the aims of the sciences and according to the objects being investigated. The full body of scientific knowledge pursues every possible aim and studies every possible object; by following such a scientific programme, Aristotle hopes to arrive at a complete account of reality. Each specific science studies a certain aspect of the world. When all of the specific sciences are assembled together, they form a unified body of knowledge that exhaustively explains reality.

There are three aims of scientific inquiry which gives rise to a threefold division of the sciences.[1] Let us examine these aims in the order in which they arose in human history. According to Aristotle, the first sciences to develop aimed at production, i.e. making things. In order to survive, human beings needed to produce certain things, and as they did, they began to acquire experience and understanding of how to produce things. These productive aims led to sciences such as agriculture, shipbuilding, carpentry and so on. Aristotle also includes among the productive sciences the fields of art and rhetoric; art is the science of producing beautiful objects and rhetoric is the science of producing fine speeches. Note then how each science can be characterized according to its aim and the objects it studies. The productive sciences all aim at making something; the objects they produce determine the specific domain of that science.

Following the emergence of the productive sciences came the practical sciences, i.e. the sciences of action. The practical sciences do not result in any physical product. Instead, these sciences aim at prescribing the means for acting well. The science that studies action with respect to individual human happiness is the science of ethics. The goal of ethics, according to Aristotle, is acting well with respect to what is good for a human being. The science of politics aims at producing excellent actions with respect to human societies and their governance. Both ethics and politics aim at fine action; they differ in that the former studies action with respect to individuals while the latter studies action with respect to societies. They thus share an aim but differ according to their objects.

Finally, once all of our basic needs were satisfied, humans could aim at something other than action or production. According to Aristotle, we began to aim at understanding and truth for no other reason than understanding; we began to seek knowledge for its own sake. Aiming at truth and understanding characterizes the theoretical sciences. In Aristotle's view, there is no loftier or nobler aim than to seek knowledge for its own sake; though theoretical sciences arose last in human history, they are the pinnacle of human scientific achievement.[2] These sciences do not aim at guiding action, nor do they aim at producing some object. Among the theoretical sciences are included the fields of logic, metaphysics, mathematics and the natural sciences. This threefold division of the sciences is represented in Figure 1. To be sure, it is entirely possible that sciences with different aims may overlap. For example, a knowledge of geometry may be of some assistance to a carpenter building a house; the carpenter and the geometer may apply some of the same ideas regarding figure. But while there is some overlap, it is clear that their goals are distinct. The geometer aims at understanding figure while the carpenter aims at the production of a house.

Let us consider some of the features of theoretical science. In Aristotle's view there are three types of entities that theoretical sciences study. First, there are entities that are separable and unchangeable. By separable, Aristotle means that these entities do not depend on anything else for their existence; they are self-subsistent and

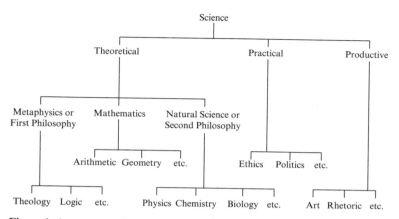

Figure 1. A representation of the structure of the sciences according to Aristotle.

capable of existing separately. For example, we need not invoke anything other than the planet to explain the existence of that planet. But for a quality such as a colour, we need to invoke something that is coloured; colour only exists insofar as there is a coloured thing. Colour is thus not self-subsistent and separable because some other thing must be invoked to explain the existence of colour. Entities such as planets, animals and others – what Aristotle calls substances – exist on their own, without invoking anything else. Unchangeable entities are those that are not subject to change; they are not generated or destroyed, nor are they modified in any way. For Aristotle, the heavenly bodies are separable and unchangeable. The heavenly bodies undergo the same circular motion for all eternity; they are also composed of an element not found in our world, i.e. the ether.[3] We now recognize that Aristotle was in error in his theory of the heavenly bodies, but it is clear what line of reasoning led him to his theory. In his view, the motion of the heavenly bodies is fundamentally different from motion on earth; the motion of heavenly bodies is in circles, whereas motion on earth is rectilinear, i.e. up and down or side-to-side. Aristotle also invoked observational evidence of the heavens to support his claim that the heavenly bodies undergo unceasing circular motions.

The theoretical science that studies separable and changeable objects is called first philosophy, or as it is now often referred to, metaphysics. From our perspective, this study of the heavenly bodies is more akin to astronomy. But there is a further feature of first philosophy that does not depend upon Aristotle's incorrect thesis about the heavenly bodies. Aristotle claims that first philosophy studies not only the heavenly bodies, but also the general nature of being or reality. In *Metaphysics Gamma (4)*, Aristotle claims that first philosophy studies being *qua* being. By this he means that first philosophy studies existing things *as* existing things; that is, first philosophy studies the things that exist and it investigates what is true of existing things simply in virtue of the fact that they exist. Linguistically speaking, first philosophy studies the various meanings of the predicate *is*; it studies the *is* of existence and the *is* of predication. First philosophy is thus the most universal and general science possible, and in Aristotle's view, all other sciences are subordinate to first philosophy. Aristotle's conception of scientific knowledge is thus clearly hierarchical; there is no more authoritative science than first philosophy; the truths of all other sciences depend on the truths of first philosophy, but first philosophy does not depend on any other science.[4]

There is also a theoretical science that studies unchangeable objects that do not exist separately. This theoretical science is mathematics. The objects of mathematics are number and figure; arithmetic is the science of number while geometry is the science of figure. The objects of mathematics are not subject to change; a three-sided figure always remains a three-sided figure, just as a number always remains the same number. Mathematical objects, however, do not exist separately. According to Aristotle, the number *three* exists only insofar as there are three things in the world; likewise with all the other numbers.[5] Figures also exist only insofar as there are things in the world that exhibit figures. Mathematical objects thus are not self-subsistent and separable; we must invoke other existing things to ensure the existence of numbers and figures. Numbers and figures exist in a way similar to attributes like colour, i.e. as qualifications and quantifications of substance. Numbers and figures thus do not exist as substances. Nevertheless, numbers and figures are real and we can attain scientific knowledge of their properties; such knowledge aims only at understanding, and so this knowledge is theoretical.

Finally, there is the science of separable and changeable entities. These entities are self-subsistent and they are subject to change. While the heavenly bodies are not subject to change, according to Aristotle, our environment on earth is the world of change. The entities of the world of change are the familiar objects of the natural world, e.g. human beings, plants, animals, rocks, etc. The theoretical science that studies these separable and changeable entities is natural science (*phusis*). Natural science includes such special disciplines as biology, botany, chemistry and physics. Aristotle often refers to natural science as second philosophy. First philosophy studies the unchangeable separable things, while second philosophy studies the changeable separable things. Mathematics is left out of this sequence because it studies derivative entities, i.e. entities that are not separable and self-subsistent. Mathematics does not study entities that are substances in the full sense; only separable and self-subsistent entities can be truly considered substances. First philosophy and second philosophy are the sciences of substances; first philosophy studies substances in the most general possible way, while second philosophy studies substances in nature.

Thus Aristotle systematizes the diverse and vast body of human knowledge. The systematic approach is guided by a focus on the aims of science and the objects under investigation. We can now understand how the structure of *Aristotle: A Guide for the Perplexed* coheres with Aristotle's views on the structure of scientific knowledge. We must begin at the beginning, which for Aristotle is first philosophy. This is the general science of being or existence and all other sciences are subordinate to it. Before we can approach any other topic in Aristotle's corpus, we must gain an understanding of the basic framework and tenets of first philosophy. This will be achieved in Chapter 2 on being or substance (*ousia*). We shall consider Aristotle's views as they are expressed in his two central works on substance: the *Categories* and the *Metaphysics*.

After first philosophy, we move on to second philosophy, i.e. natural science. Here our primary text is the first two books of the *Physics*. In this work, Aristotle explains the first principles of nature. He introduces his well-known theory of the four causes that the student of nature must understand. This is also where Aristotle develops his best defence of his view that everything in nature is directed at some end or goal (*telos*). Aristotle rejects purely mechanistic explanations in the natural world; the natural world must be explained also in terms of the goals or ends of the natural entities. In first philosophy, we study being and existence generally; in second philosophy, we study a specific kind of being, i.e. the existence of entities in the world of change.

For Aristotle, the single most important distinction in the natural world is between that which lives and that which does not. Life will thus form our next subject. Aristotle was a biologist through and through; he was keenly interested in living things. Indeed, his biological writings form the largest portion of his work. For Aristotle, it is the presence of the soul that explains the life of a thing. Thus in exploring these issues about life, we shall explore his account of the soul. Our primary text here will be *De Anima*, or *On the Soul*. Our course of study will thus trace three theoretical sciences: first philosophy, second philosophy, and the philosophy of soul.

Finally, after studying Aristotle's account of the soul and life in general, we shall undertake an investigation of human life and human happiness. This is the science of ethics and our primary text here will be the *Nicomachean Ethics*. This is the only practical science that we will explore in this book. Ethics is the science of producing excellent actions that lead to human happiness or flourishing, what the Greeks called *eudaimonia*. Here Aristotle develops his famous account of the virtues and he explores various conceptions of the good life for human beings.

There is thus a specific logic for the course of study offered in this book: we begin with the general science of being; we then move on to the science of nature; within the science of nature we examine life or soul; finally, within the science of life, we examine human life. We can be thankful to Aristotle for assisting our inquiry by providing this clear and reasoned structure of scientific knowledge. If we ever feel lost in exploring the vast range of human knowledge, we can always orient ourselves by asking what is our aim and what is our object. With those questions answered, we will know not only what science we are pursuing, but also how that science fits within the vast body of human knowledge.

DEMONSTRATION (*APODEIXIS*)

Not only does scientific knowledge exhibit a specific structure, but it also exhibits a specific character. Before we can begin a study of the specific sciences treated in this book, we must first develop an understanding of the formal characteristics of scientific knowledge. For Aristotle, science is not a collection of facts, but rather a series of *explanations*; we have scientific knowledge when we understand the reason why something is the case. Rather than viewing science as a mere collection of facts, Aristotle views science as a series of causally connected facts. The precise character of these explanations is an important subject for Aristotle. Logic aims at consistency, but science aims at truth as well as consistency. We want to arrive at truth through science, and further, we want to know that we have attained truth. In order to ensure truth, Aristotle develops his notion of demonstration (*apodeixis*); demonstration is the focal point of Aristotle's formal discussion of scientific knowledge. We have scientific knowledge when we can provide a demonstration of the hypothesis at hand. Our main text for this formal discussion of scientific knowledge is the *Posterior Analytics*.[6]

In developing a conception of demonstrative or axiomatic science, Aristotle takes Euclidean geometry as his model; though Euclid's work was done after Aristotle's death, Euclid's predecessors had already made substantial progress in developing an axiomatic conception of geometry. An axiomatic or demonstrative science is one in which a few basic premises are accepted as truths; all further truths of the science are established through deductive means by appeal to the basic axioms. This method of proof is called a demonstration. If we know that our axioms are true, and if we have truth-preserving rules of logical deduction, then we know that anything that we derive from our axioms is true. It was Aristotle's belief that this axiomatic method that had proved so fruitful for geometry would also enable the progress and development of all other fields.

Let us also note that Aristotle shared this axiomatic conception of science with Plato, but each philosopher offered distinct versions of axiomatic science. For Plato, all scientific knowledge could be founded upon a single set of axioms. These axioms would invoke knowledge of the eternal and immutable Forms.[7] From this single set of axioms, all knowledge could be deduced. We can call Plato's view on this point a strongly unitary conception of axiomatic science. Plato's view on the vast body of human knowledge is that all knowledge is part of a single unified science. Aristotle, however, seems to have been much more impressed by the diversity and distinctness of different sciences. Sciences can have different aims, different objects and different methods by which they pursue those aims and objects. Aristotle thus maintained that each specific discipline has its own set of axioms and that these axioms are not reducible to some overarching single set of axioms. Ethics, for example, has its own axioms, and these axioms cannot be reduced to the axioms of some other science. Aristotle considered it unlikely that scientific disciplines as different as ethics and geometry, for example, would subscribe to a single set of axioms.[8] For Aristotle, then, the body of scientific knowledge is a connected plurality; science is not strongly unitary in the sense that Plato maintained, but there is a weaker sense of the unity of scientific knowledge.

Now that we have seen Aristotle's view on the structure of demonstrative science, let us examine in greater detail the characteristics of demonstration. Aristotle states, 'by demonstration I mean a scientific deduction; and by scientific I mean one in virtue of which, by having it, we understand something' (71b17–19). Aristotle is here contrasting a scientific deduction with a logical deduction. All deductions are performed according to the form of a syllogism; Aristotle is credited with the development of the syllogism and indeed with the invention of logic.[9] A formal logical deduction is one in which we can recognize validity, but we do not thereby understand something by it. Formal logical deductions are made without any reference to content, i.e. to what the deduction is about. Scientific deductions, however, are deductions in which we can recognize validity and through which we understand something about the world. Demonstrations thus do not merely describe observable phenomena; demonstrations explain the reason why an observable phenomenon occurs. Aristotle states, 'we understand a thing *simpliciter* . . . whenever we think we are aware both that the explanation because of which the object is is its explanation, and it is not possible for this to be otherwise' (71b9–11). In addition to offering an explanation, demonstrations also explain why things must be this way and no other. This feature of demonstration is often referred to as the necessity condition: we have scientific knowledge when we know why something necessarily must be this way and no other. The former feature is often referred to as the causality condition. Note that Aristotle's word for *explanation* (*aitia*) also means *cause*. We have scientific knowledge when we perform a deduction that satisfies both the causality condition and the necessity condition: we understand why something is the way it is, and we understand that it must be this way and no other.

Scientific explanations also aspire to universality. Aristotle connects the universality of scientific explanations with the necessity condition: 'I call universal whatever belongs to something both of every case and in itself as such. It is evident, therefore, that whatever is universal belongs from necessity to its objects' (73b25–27). Scientific claims are thus generalizations; they highlight the orderly patterns of nature. Scientific claims are not claims about particular objects, e.g. Socrates or Callias. Rather, scientific claims are about universal terms that belong of necessity to their objects, e.g. humans are rational and mammals have parents. These are necessary and universal truths. Scientific knowledge thus enables us to see particulars, e.g. Socrates and Callias among others, as part of a general pattern. Scientific knowledge must be formulated in terms of these universal, necessary and general patterns; scientific knowledge cannot be formulated in terms of particular entities.

Scientific knowledge thus seeks necessity and universality in its explanations. While these are lofty ideals for scientific achievement, we should note the ways in which these ideals conflict with the practice of science. Aristotle's conditions here seem to rule out that we could ever have scientific knowledge of contingent facts, i.e. things that happened to be this way but just as well could have happened to be another way. If science were concerned with necessity, then contingent facts would fall outside of the bounds of science. Likewise with universality. The above example concerning the rationality of human beings does have exceptions; there are some individuals who from defect of birth do not possess human rationality. Many general scientific claims have such exceptions. It is best to understand both the universality and the necessity conditions as being part of the aims and aspirations of science. Aristotle is setting forth the goal; science should strive for generality and necessity as far as possible. It may not always be possible to strictly adhere to these goals. We may need to account for contingent facts. Aristotle himself does back away from the strictness of the universality requirements, saying that science indicates patterns that happen always or for the most part. Thus science investigates general patterns, but not only patterns that obtain without exception.

There is yet another way in which Aristotle's description of scientific knowledge reflects his ideals about science. Those who have practised science will know that few scientists are busy with deductions and demonstrations. Aristotle is thus vulnerable to a serious objection: whatever he has described, it is not the actual practice of scientific inquiry. Aristotle was aware of this objection and he developed a response to it. The axiomatic science described by Aristotle is not meant as a description of how scientists actually work; rather, it is a description of how the results of scientific inquiry should be presented. Aristotle distinguishes between the order of explanation and the order of discovery in science. Discovery occurs through the observation of particular phenomena that are then generalized into patterns. We can view this process as proceeding from the bottom up; from observable phenomena, scientists develop general hypotheses and test those hypotheses. This is the everyday work of scientists. We can imagine, Aristotle says, a point at which scientific inquiry is completed. When our inquiries are completed, Aristotle asks, how should the findings of science be presented? The answer is clear: a completed science should be presented as an axiomatic system, with basic premises and with all further truths of the science following in deductive fashion from the axioms, hypotheses and definitions. This is of course not how scientists actually work; but when their work is done, this is how their work should be presented. While the order of discovery proceeds from the bottom up, the order of explanation proceeds from the top down. The necessity and universality conditions as well as the demonstrative structure of science thus all represent the ideal of achievement in science. The actual practice of science is often sporadic and halting; but the completed sciences will all exhibit a demonstrative character as well as aspirations to necessity and universality.

THE AXIOMS OF THE SCIENCES

The axioms are the starting points for demonstration; they are thus the foundations for demonstrative science. Aristotle describes several characteristics of the axioms; some of these characteristics are obvious, though others are more difficult to grasp. In this section we will survey Aristotle's account of the axioms and their role in demonstrative science; we will also attend to some of the philosophical difficulties of his account.

Concerning the axioms, Aristotle states, 'it is necessary for demonstrative understanding in particular to depend on things which are true and primitive and immediate and more familiar than and prior to and explanatory of the conclusion' (72b21–22). Let us treat each of these characteristics. It is obvious that the axioms must be true; they cannot be known unless they are true, nor can they serve as the basis for scientific knowledge unless they are true. The axioms must also be primitive and immediate. By this Aristotle means that the nothing can be more basic than the axioms. The axioms must be immediate in the sense that our knowledge of them is not mediated by anything else; there are no propositions prior to the axioms that mediate our understanding of the axioms. The axioms are thus primitive and immediate in the sense that they are basic and that our knowledge of them is direct and unmediated. To emphasize these characteristics, Aristotle sometimes refers to axioms as primitives and immediates.

The remaining characteristics describe the axioms with relation to the conclusion reached through a scientific deduction. The axioms serve as the premises of a deduction, and Aristotle states that the axioms must be more familiar than the conclusion, prior to the conclusion and explanatory of the conclusion. The axioms must be explanatory of the conclusion because 'we only understand when we know the explanation' (71b30). This characteristic thus draws upon Aristotle's conception of scientific knowledge as explanatory. Aristotle also contends that the axioms must be more familiar than and prior to the conclusion. By this he means that we cannot be better convinced of the truth of the conclusion than we are of the premises. The truth of the conclusion depends upon the truth of the premises; our logic would indeed be inverted if we had more confidence in the truth of the conclusion than in the truth of the premises. To clarify this point, Aristotle distinguishes between things that are familiar and prior *to us* and things that are familiar and prior *by nature* (72a1–5). Those things that are familiar and prior to us are the objects of perception. Those things that are familiar and prior by nature are the universals, which are furthest from the senses; these are by nature the most knowable things. In the order of explanation, these universals that are furthest from the senses are prior and more familiar. The axioms are familiar and prior in this latter sense; in the order of explanation, then, there is nothing more familiar than or prior to the axioms.

There remains one key feature of the axioms: 'it is necessary for these immediates to be non-demonstrable' (72b23). The axioms are the basis for all demonstrative knowledge, but the axioms themselves cannot be known through demonstration. If everything were demonstrable, Aristotle argues, then our demonstrations would lead to an infinite regress. In demonstrating one proposition, we would appeal back to a further proposition that can be demonstrated, and so on into infinity. There would be no point at which our demonstrations would stop. For Aristotle this produces a serious difficulty, for we are not capable of grasping the infinite. If scientific demonstrations were characterized by an infinite regress, then scientific knowledge would be in a crucial sense unknowable. This is clearly an unsatisfactory result. Aristotle also considers the possibility that demonstrations may 'come about in a circle and reciprocally' (72b19). This, however, is also unacceptable because in this case our demonstrations will be circular; premises will depend on the conclusions they are supposed to prove. This would run afoul of the requirement that the axioms must be more familiar than and prior to the conclusion; in a circular argument, the axioms would be both more familiar and prior to the conclusion as well as less familiar and posterior. In order to avoid the infinite regress and the circularity that would ruin our scientific knowledge, Aristotle maintains that it is necessary that the axioms are non-demonstrable.

For demonstrative knowledge, it is necessary that there be starting points. Demonstration must thus come to a stop at some point; demonstration cannot go on into infinity. Demonstration is only possible, then, if the starting points are known without demonstration.[10] This raises a difficult issue for Aristotle, for scientific knowledge has explicitly been defined as a demonstration through which we understand something. If the axioms are not known demonstratively, then they are not strictly speaking known in the same way as the rest of the body of scientific knowledge. For Aristotle, everything in science is known demonstratively except the axioms. It remains for Aristotle then to explain how exactly we know the axioms.

Aristotle takes up this topic in Chapter 19 of Book 2 of the *Posterior Analytics*. His stated goal is to explain 'how they [the axioms] become familiar and what is the state that becomes familiar with them' (99b18). Aristotle begins by laying out the puzzles of this topic; in doing so, he addresses the claim that the axioms are not known and cannot become known. Aristotle rightly sees this claim as disastrous for his scientific enterprise. If the axioms are not known already and cannot become known, then scientific knowledge based on the axioms is impossible. One possible solution is that we already possess knowledge of the axioms. Perhaps we are born with this innate knowledge, as Plato argued.[11] But if we are born with this knowledge, we are not aware of it. Aristotle claims that it is absurd to suppose that we have knowledge of the axioms innately and yet this somehow escapes our notice; the axioms are the highest kind of knowledge, and it seems to Aristotle extremely unlikely that we could possess innate knowledge of the axioms and yet be unaware of this knowledge. But if we do not already possess this knowledge innately, how can we ever acquire it? We cannot acquire it through demonstration, as has already been shown. We cannot acquire knowledge of the axioms from pre-existing knowledge, since there is nothing that is prior to the axioms. We are then left with a puzzle: we do not have innate knowledge of the axioms, nor do we have the means to acquire such knowledge.

Aristotle's solution to this puzzle focuses on the innate capacity for perception. While all animals are capable of perceiving, for some animals perceptions are retained and become part of the animal's memory. From memory comes experience,

> and from experience, or from the whole universal that has come to rest in the soul . . . there comes a principle of understanding – of skill if it deals with how things come about, of understanding if it deals with what is the case . . . Thus it is clear that it is necessary for us to become familiar with the primitives by induction; for perception too instills the universal in this way. (100a5–9, 100b4–5)

Aristotle here describes the process by which we form universal concepts; these universal concepts are the elements of the axioms. The axioms are universal statements about the subject at hand. Thus while the axioms are formulated in terms of universal concepts, these concepts arise in us through perception, memory and experience of particulars. In this way Aristotle's account of our familiarity with the axioms is inductive; it is based upon our experience of particulars. From enough experience of particulars we form a universal concept that becomes part of an axiom. Consider how Aristotle's account explains the following example. It is an axiom of biology that all living things die. We are not born with knowledge of this axiom; it is not innate in us. Nor do we know this axiom through demonstration. Rather, we know it because we perceive over and over again that particular living things die. From these perceptions of particular deaths of living things, we form memories and experiences. Ultimately these experiences lead us to the formation of the concept of mortality. We come to recognize the universal in the particulars and this leads us to the certainty of the axiom: all living things die.

There is a specific intellectual state through which we know the axioms. This state is not understanding, for understanding involves giving an account or a demonstration. Knowledge of the axioms is the most precise and certain kind of knowledge, so the intellectual state must be more certain and precise than understanding. Our knowledge of the axioms is achieved through the state of *nous*. How to translate this term is a controversial matter. *Nous* is generally used to refer to *mind* or *intellect*, but here Aristotle gives it a specific and technical meaning. We might render this state of *nous* through which we know the axioms as *comprehension* or *intuition*. However we elect to translate this term, the key point is that *nous* is distinct from understanding; *nous* does not involve knowing something demonstratively. *Nous* is grounded in induction, but this state achieves the highest degree of certainty and precision possible.

Such is Aristotle's account of how the axioms 'become familiar and what is the state that becomes familiar with them' (99b18). Almost as soon as Aristotle provided this account it was met with objections. Aristotle has provided an account of how we form universal concepts, but it still seems that there is a gap between universal concept formation and grasping the necessary truth of the axioms. It has been suggested that the faculty of *nous* somehow fills this gap. Some have even accused Aristotle of a residual Platonism; Aristotle's account seems to depend upon an innate ability to receive universal concepts and recognize necessary truths. It seems that there is more than perception, memory and experience at work in this process. Some have maintained that such an appeal to Platonism flatly contradicts Aristotle's empirical and inductive approach. While there are significant philosophical issues still unresolved, the foregoing discussion has presented the broad outlines of Aristotle's account and the difficulties it faces.

In this chapter, we have laid out the foundations of Aristotle's view of scientific knowledge. We have reached an understanding of the structure of scientific knowledge; that structure is guided by questions about the aims and the objects of a particular scientific inquiry. We have also examined the basic features of Aristotle's demonstrative science. Through this we have achieved an understanding of how the findings of science should be presented, as well as the ideals to which demonstrative science should aspire. Finally, we examined the nature of our knowledge of the axioms upon which all demonstrative knowledge depends. This understanding of

Aristotle's view of scientific knowledge is vital for pursuing our course of study in the next several chapters. With an understanding of what science in general seeks, we can now turn to four specific sciences: 1) first philosophy or metaphysics, 2) second philosophy or natural science, 3) the account of soul, which is a part of the science of biology, and 4) the practical science of human happiness.

CHAPTER 2

BEING OR SUBSTANCE (*OUSIA*)

And indeed the question that, both now and of old, has always been raised, and has always been the subject of doubt, *what is being?* – is just the question, *what is substance?*" (1028b4–5)

Many of Aristotle's inquiries begin with a childlike innocence and wonder; Aristotle is near enough to the beginnings of philosophy to voice amazement at the nature of reality. While his subsequent inquiry into the question of being is often difficult, sophisticated and subtle, we would do well to remember the simple origin of his investigation. He is concerned here with a basic and fundamental question, one that previous philosophers have asked and puzzled about: what is real? This is not just a philosopher's question; this question reflects a universal human curiosity about the world we inhabit. Many of us may have gazed up at the heavens and pondered the nature of reality. Aristotle's starting point is thus not some obscure philosophical issue; instead he begins with a simple question that any human being may ask. As we discover, however, a simple question can be exceedingly difficult to answer. But before we move on to the complexities of Aristotle's attempts to understand being, we should keep in mind the simple yet profound question that launches our inquiry.

This question about being is the most general question that can be asked about reality. Aristotle is not here asking what it means to be a human, or a tree, or a heavenly body; he is instead asking what it means to *simply be anything*. We assume that there are real things around us, but what entitles us to conclude that something is real? What are we saying when we declare that something is real? What explains the reality of the things that are? What is true of something simply in virtue of the fact that it exists? What is the structure of reality? Do all things that are real exist in the same way, or are some things more real or basic than others? We now can begin to see how our simple original question opens up several vexing issues. These issues surrounding being form the branch of philosophy called ontology, which means the *study of being*. While the terms *being* and *reality* are widely accepted translations of the Greek terms *ousia* and *einai*, we should note that the philosophical term *substance* is also often used to render these Greek terms. All three of these English terms indicate a similar philosophical meaning: *being*, *reality* and *substance* are all ways of expressing the true underlying nature or essence of a thing. It is this underlying nature or essence that Aristotle is so keen to investigate and explain.

A further clarification regarding this study of being is necessary. One might suspect that in studying being, one studies some transcendent or overarching being; one might conclude that there is something out there to investigate, namely that which is being. On this view, ontology studies the entity in the universe that is *being*. This, however, is not Aristotle's approach. There is no transcendent *being* out there in the universe; instead, there are simply *beings*, i.e. particular existing things. Reality is composed of particular things; these beings are real substances, according to Aristotle. If we wish to investigate and understand *being* in general, we must do so by investigating the reality and nature of particular existing *beings*. This distinction is subtle but crucial for understanding Aristotle's approach.

Aristotle's approach to these questions about being and substance reveals much about his way of doing philosophy. There are two main features of Aristotle's method that I would like to highlight. First, for Aristotle, progress is achieved by considering the opinions and theories of other great minds that have tackled these questions; only then can we hope to surpass their understanding of the subject. Second, Aristotle's thought reflects a remarkable tendency to systematize and categorize. In our attempt to understand Aristotle's concerns about being, we will see evidence of both of these tendencies.

As the quote that begins this chapter indicates, Aristotle acknowledges that he is not the first to have wondered about being; this is an issue with a long history, and it would be a great disservice to his predecessors to ignore their attempts to understand being. Aristotle often begins by surveying the reputable opinions held by his predecessors; he also lays out the puzzles or confusions that befell his predecessors. We shall see this approach in almost every one of Aristotle's writings. There are a number of reasons why Aristotle would employ this method. It is generally agreed among scholars that most of Aristotle's writings were not prepared for publication but are instead his lecture notes. A survey of earlier thought is indispensable in any lecture course; for Aristotle to offer a comprehensive education to his students, he must offer an examination of the theories of other experts. Understanding the history of a subject is instrumental to mastering a subject. To investigate being, Aristotle thus draws upon the theories and opinions offered by earlier generations of philosophers and he explores the difficulties into which their theories fell. Aristotle does not just undertake this survey as an historical exercise; he has tremendous respect and admiration for the work of earlier scientists and philosophers. He surveys earlier work on the subject because it offers the possibility for the advancement of his own investigations; we need not begin anew when generations of the brightest intellects of Greece have offered serious theories for consideration. It may turn out that the earlier theories have a great deal of truth to them; perhaps the puzzles that thwarted earlier philosophers can be resolved. Aristotle is never dismissive toward the theories of his predecessors; he may reject earlier theories, but only after thoughtful consideration. Though Aristotle certainly ranks as one of the most brilliant and intellectually ambitious individuals who have ever lived, he was not above learning from others.

BEING BEFORE ARISTOTLE

There are two main approaches offered by Aristotle's predecessors, and we shall treat each of them in turn. Aristotle's own thought reflects a profound engagement with the theories of his predecessors. His predecessors fall into two main camps: the Presocratic philosophers and Plato. In general, the former developed a materialist account of being, while Plato developed an idealist account of being. Aristotle found both of these approaches to be deeply problematic, and he offers numerous arguments and considerations that lead him to reject these approaches. Aristotle does not, however, roundly dismiss these approaches. While he considers the materialist and idealist approaches inadequate, he does retain certain aspects of these theories. It is thus helpful to view Aristotle as charting a middle course between the materialist and idealist approaches to being and substance. The resulting account of being proposed by Aristotle can thus be viewed as the culmination of ancient Greek thought on being.

Let us first consider the theories of the Presocratic philosophers. The Presocratic philosophers were a group of theorists active in the sixth and fifth centuries BC; these men are almost universally credited with inventing philosophy and science. Though they inhabited different parts of the ancient Greek world, in many cases they were aware of each other's theories and hypotheses. They thus offered criticisms of rival theories; in this respect they formed the earliest known scientific community in human history. Up to this point I have been referring to Aristotle's predecessors as philosophers, but we must be aware that the extension of that term was wider in the ancient world than it is now. Aristotle called the Presocratic thinkers *phusikoi*, which means *students of nature*. The Presocratics pondered questions of chemistry, biology and cosmology as well as questions of speculative philosophy. There were no divisions among academic disciplines to restrain the theories of these earliest philosopher/ scientists. For them, questions about reality transcended such boundaries. We thus find their thoughts covering diverse subjects and phenomena.

Nearly every one of the Presocratic philosophers was deeply concerned with the origin of cosmos and the laws of nature, respectively cosmogony and cosmology. The key Greek term for these Presocratics is *arche*, which means *beginning* or *origin*. The Latin word *principium*, which means *principle*, is also often used as a rendering of *arche*. The Presocratics thus sought the origins of the world, or what we might call the first principle of nature. They did not understand questions of origin exclusively in a temporal sense, though, to be sure, they did inquire as to when and how the universe began. The *arche*, then, would explain how the universe began. The *arche* would also explain what the universe is based upon, i.e. what is the foundation or first principle of the order of the universe. The *arche* thus should explain both how the universe began and what it is at its most basic level. Recall the core meaning of *arche*: a beginning. The universe has a beginning in time and it has a beginning in terms of how it is explained. When we try to give a theory of the universe, there is some part of that theory that would have to come first; this is what the Presocratics sought in the *arche*.

In general, the Presocratics sought the *arche* in matter, i.e. the basic elemental stuff of the universe such as earth, air, water and fire. The Eleatic philosophers Parmenides, Melissus and Zeno fall outside of this general trend in Presocratic thought, and their views will be considered along with those of Plato. For now let us consider the materialist views of the Presocratics. Several of the Presocratics were both materialists and monists, i.e. they held that the *arche* is one type of matter, whether earth, air, water or fire. Consider the views of the first *phusikos*, Thales, who held that 'all is water'.[1] It is difficult to interpret this claim. Thales may mean that everything that is comes from water; all plants, animals, rocks and indeed everything finds its origin in water. This at least is how Aristotle interpreted Thales' view. It is also possible to interpret Thales as claiming that everything that is not only comes from water, but also actually is water at this very moment. Even though a person or a plant seems to be made of other elemental stuffs, it really is made of just water of varying densities or temperatures. On this latter view, Thales is offering an account not only of the origins of the universe, but also of the present state of the universe.

Several other Presocratic philosophers offer a similar approach, though they settle on a different element or collection of elements as the *arche*. Anaximenes, for example, argued that all objects are really just varying densities of air. Empedocles offered a pluralist theory of the *arche*; rather than settling on one element, he argued that all four elements should be regarded as the *arche*. The atomists Leucippus and Democritus proposed the view that the *arche* consisted of indivisible material particles called *atoms*, which literally means *that which cannot be cut*. These Presocratic thinkers thus present theories that explain what the universe is at its most basic and fundamental level: it is a particular elemental material that underlies all the familiar objects of our world. This underlying material is also referred to as the substratum (*hypokeimenon*), which means *that which underlies* or *the underlying thing*. If you seek to explain what a human being is, or what a plant or rock is, then your explanation will begin with the fact that the object in question is composed of an underlying material, i.e. a substratum. The elemental matter also persists in a way that familiar objects such as plants or animals do not. This plant or that animal comes into being and is destroyed; the elemental matter is not destroyed; it merely takes on different arrangements. This is another reason why the Presocratics regarded elemental matter as the *arche*.

We can note the similarity between this materialist approach of the *phusikoi* and the contemporary state of the natural sciences. While our elemental charts may be more complex and accurate than those of the earliest scientists, the theoretical approaches are similar. Physicists search for the most basic stuff of the universe, and they seek this in matter. Physicists have not yet determined whether this matter will be of one type, i.e. monistic, or of several types, i.e. pluralistic; but most physicists are confident that at the subatomic level we will someday discover the fundamental material particles of which everything in the universe is composed. If this fundamental material is ever discovered, any explanation of an object in the universe will begin with the claim that the object is made of material *x*. The arrangements of material *x* may be complex and extremely varied, but everything is made of *x*. While the theories of the *phusikoi* may share these similarities with contemporary science, we shall find that Aristotle was largely unimpressed by attempts to find the fundamental explanation of being in matter. It will prove instructive to explore Aristotle's arguments against a materialist theory of being.

While the general tendency of the Presocratics was to seek the foundation of being in elemental matter, Plato sought the basis of reality in the immaterial. Deeply influenced by the Presocratic philosopher Parmenides, Plato rejected the notion that the basis of reality could be found in matter. The material world is subject to change; objects come into being and pass away; and the elements that compose objects take on one conformation after another. For Plato, the prevalence of change in the material world implied that there could be no eternal knowledge of the material realm; if we seek lasting and permanent knowledge, then we must seek such knowledge among the parts of our world that are not subject to change. Plato thus develops his theory of Forms, i.e. changeless intelligible entities such as Justice, Equality and Beauty.[2] These entities are universals; the Form of Beauty covers all the beautiful objects in the world; conversely, all beautiful objects share in or participate in the Form of Beauty. It is this participation in the Form of Beauty that makes beautiful things beautiful. But while beautiful objects are subject to change, the Form of Beauty is eternal and changeless. For Plato, the material world is thus in an important sense illusory or misleading; material objects are imperfect instantiations of the universal Forms. The material world is also dependent in a way that the world of Forms is not; a beautiful object must share in the Form of Beauty in order to be beautiful; but the Form of Beauty exists and is knowable regardless of whether any actual beautiful objects exist. If we want to gain eternal knowledge, we must direct our attention away from the illusory material world to the world of the Forms. The world of the Forms is thus more real than the material world. If we seek to explain any of the material objects we sense, we can only do so by appealing to the changeless Forms.

These two opposing tendencies lay the groundwork for Aristotle's approach to being. The Presocratic tendency is to seek being in the sub-sensible, i.e. the elemental material of which sensible objects are composed. Plato's approach pays little heed to the evidence of the senses; he seeks the nature of reality in the realm beyond the senses, what we shall call the super-sensible. Notice how both of these approaches suggest that the world is not the way it appears to our senses. Though it may seem that plants, human beings and countless other sensible objects are the real entities of the world, the Presocratics and Plato argue that this information from the senses masks the true nature of reality. For the Presocratics, the world revealed by the senses consists of everyday objects that are generated and destroyed; these everyday objects are thus impermanent and could not serve as the *arche*. Plato's concern with the impermanence of everyday objects led him to turn to the changeless Forms as the basis of reality. Though they take different philosophical directions, both the Presocratics and Plato are motivated by a similar concern regarding the impermanence of the world of the senses. Thus the truth about being is to be found either in the elemental constituents of sensible objects or in the universal forms that are not sensible but are intelligible.

Against this backdrop, Aristotle's theory of being concludes that reality is largely the way it appears to the senses. It seems to the senses that the basic elements of reality are the everyday objects we encounter, e.g. this man, that tree, etc. The world seems to be composed of a plurality of separable and self-subsistent substances. Aristotle's challenge is to demonstrate that the way things *seem* to the senses is the way things actually *are*. The fact that Aristotle maintains that reality is the way it appears to the senses has led many of his interpreters to conclude that his philosophical approach appeals to common sense. A person with little philosophical experience may hold a theory of being that states that sensible everyday objects are the real and basic constituents of the world. While the Presocratics and Plato may challenge this view, ultimately Aristotle agrees with the common-sense view of the everyday person in the street. But rather than merely settling for a philosophically unsophisticated view, Aristotle provides the philosophical justification for the common-sense approach to being.

BEING IN THE *CATEGORIES*

Aristotle's theory of being is first developed in the *Categories*.[3] The *Categories* is probably the best text with which to begin any serious study of Aristotle. Later editors compiled the *Categories* and four other texts into what became known as the *Organon*. *Organon* is the Latin word for *tool* or *instrument*.[4] It is believed that editors compiled these five texts because they all deal with matters of logic; logic is the instrument or tool through which we can assess the validity of our statements about reality. While it is appropriate to consider the *Categories* in this logical context, the inquiry undertaken in the *Categories* is significant for ontology and metaphysics as well. Even though this text is brief, it can be difficult to grasp Aristotle's approach and his concerns about being in this text. The background material on the Presocratic and Platonic theories of being is intended to provide the philosophical context for understanding Aristotle's attempt to get clear on being. If we can also keep in mind the simple philosophical musings with which Aristotle begins, we shall be well positioned to extract the philosophical significance of this short but profound text.

Let us first be clear on the meaning of the title. *Categories* is a translation of the Greek word *kategoria*, which means both *category* and *predicate* or *predication*. The *Categories* is structured as we might infer from this dual meaning of the title: Aristotle categorizes and classifies the different kinds of predicates that are used in our speech. This dual meaning of the title thus suggests a particular philosophical method: Aristotle investigates being by first investigating our utterances. By examining the types of statements that we make and by categorizing those types of statements, Aristotle reveals the underlying structure of reality presupposed by our utterances. In classifying predicates, then, we classify things. We must keep in mind the distinction between our utterances about objects and the objects themselves; language about objects and the objects themselves are not the same things. Language is a way of signifying the things themselves. In places, Aristotle slides between these linguistic and ontological approaches. What begins as a linguistic exercise thus turns out to have crucial ontological implications. Note how this method is revealed in Aristotle's text. Chapter 2 of the *Categories* begins with a telling phrase: 'of things that are said' (1a16). Aristotle goes on to classify *the things that are said*, and in doing so, his theory of *the things that are* emerges.

Aristotle begins with a fourfold classification of the things that are said. It is vital to be clear on this classification, for it guides much of Aristotle's reasoning in this text. This fourfold classification turns upon two critical notions: things that are *said of* a subject and things that are *in* a subject. These terms indicate that there are two basic ways in which we can predicate with respect to any given subject. Given that there are these two basic forms of predication, and a predicate can either exhibit or lack one or both of these forms of predication, this gives rise to four possibilities: 1) a predicate that is *said of* a subject but is not *in* a subject; 2) a predicate that is *in* a subject but is not *said of* a subject; 3) a predicate that is both *in* a subject and *said of* a subject; and finally, 4) a form of speech that is neither *said of* a subject nor *in* a subject. This last category is crucial for Aristotle's inquiry; this form of speech is not a predicate, for it is neither said of nor in a subject; given that there are only two ways of predicating, and the last category fulfils neither, it follows that the last category is not a predicate. As Aristotle argues, that which is neither said of nor in a subject can only serve as a subject for predication, but it can never serve as a predicate.

Let us examine these forms of predication more closely. Consider first what it means for something to be *in* a subject. Aristotle tells us that 'By "in a subject" I mean what is in something, not as a part, and cannot exist separately from what it is in' (1a24). There are two key points in this explanation. First is what we shall call the separateness criterion, i.e. that for something to be in a subject it cannot exist separately from the subject it is in. This means that what is in a subject is in a crucial sense dependent on the subject; what is in a subject can only exist insofar as it is in a subject. Aristotle's example of the colour white will help to clarify this point. Considered linguistically, this means that in order to predicate qualities like colour, there must be a subject of that predication. It is the nature of language that in order for there to be a predication there must be a subject. From this linguistic point Aristotle derives an ontological conclusion about objects and their properties. In order for the colour white to exist, it must exist in a thing, i.e. there must be a thing that is coloured white. If there is no thing, then there can be no colour at all. In other words, qualities like colour do not float freely in the universe; qualities must be grounded in things. Inhering in an object is what makes qualities like colour real. Were there no things, there could be no colour.

Aristotle also says that by *in a subject* he means what is in something not as a part. This means that things like a hand or a leaf on a tree do not count as being in a subject; these items are part of a subject rather than qualities of a subject. This distinction is well founded and appeals to our intuitions. The relationship of a hand to a body is importantly different from the relationship of the colour white to a body. Paleness is in Socrates, but Socrates' hand is not in his body; rather it is a part of his body.

The kinds of predicates that are in a subject are qualities, quantities and relations (1b25). These predicates are attributes of a subject. Each of these must be in a subject; they cannot exist separately. It is empty to speak of quantity unless one is quantifying a subject; likewise, one cannot speak of relations unless there is a relation of one or more subjects. Aristotle goes on to compile a list of nine specific forms of predication of substance: 1) of quantity, 2) of quality, 3) of relation, 4) of place where, 5) of time when, 6) of being in a position, 7) of having or possessing, 8) of doing, 9) of being affected. Collectively, we shall refer to these forms of predication as *attributes*. Attributes are not separable or self-subsistent; they are derivative entities. When substance is added to this list of nine attributes, we arrive at Aristotle's doctrine of the ten categories. Do not put too much stock in this specific list of ten, however; Aristotle was not committed to exactly ten categories. In other texts he presents fewer than ten categories. Whether we choose to adopt ten or fewer categories, the core feature of his view is that the world is divisible into subjects and ways of predicating those subjects, i.e. substances and attributes.

While attributes are all in a subject, there is one additional form of predication that is *said of* a subject but is not in a subject. Aristotle presents the example of the predicating *human being* of an individual person. This gives rise to a statement of the following form: Socrates is a human being. Aristotle tells us that the predicate *human being* is not *in* Socrates; rather, the predicate *human being* describes what kind of a thing Socrates is. Consider Aristotle's explanation: 'if something is said of a subject both its name and its definition are necessarily predicated of the subject' (2a19–20). This is a key point, for predicates that are in a subject never have their definition predicated of the subject. Consider again the example of Socrates, who happens to be white. The definition of white is the following: reflected light of a certain wavelength. The definition of a human being is the following: a rational animal. Now try to substitute each of these definitions into the sentence *Socrates is x*. For the latter predicate, this would result in the following sentence: Socrates is a rational animal. This is a true predication with respect to Socrates. With the former predicate, the following sentence results: Socrates is reflected light of a certain wavelength. This is a flatly false predication with respect to Socrates; he is not light of a certain wavelength. He is a human being whose body reflects light of a certain wavelength. What Aristotle illustrates here are two fundamentally different ways of predicating with respect to any given subject. A predicate that is *in* a subject cannot have its definition predicated of the subject; a predicate that is *said of* a subject necessarily has its definition predicated of the subject. Attributes thus never have their definitions predicated of a subject. A subject *is not* a quality, a quantity or a relation; rather, a subject *has* qualities, quantities and relations. But a subject *is* what is *said of* that subject.

Predicates that are *said of* a subject thus have a specific and unique relationship to a subject: predicates that are *said of* a subject describe *what kind of a thing* the subject is. Aristotle tells us that the predicates that are *said of* a subject are species and genus terms, e.g. human being, plant, animal, mammal, etc. We should also note that species and genus terms are universal terms; the term *human being* describes each of the individual members of the species. Predicates that are *said of* a subject describe what kind of a thing the subject is, while predicates that are *in* a subject describe attributes of the subject. Predicates that are *said of* a subject are thus vastly more informative than predicates about qualities, quantities or relations of a subject: 'It is reasonable that, after the primary substances, their species and genera should be the only other things called substances. For only they, of things predicated, reveal the primary substance' (2b29–30). Because predicates that are *said of* a subject answer the question 'what kind of a thing is this?' Aristotle states that such predicates must be regarded as *secondary substance*. Before we examine this notion of secondary substance, let us look at the other half of Aristotle's fourfold classification.

We have seen how some predicates are *in* a subject but not *said of* any subject, and we have seen how other predicates are *said of* a subject but not *in* any subject. There is also a class of predicates that are both *in* a subject and *said of* a subject. At first this class of predicates may seem confusing given that *said of* and *in* present two completely different ways of relating to a subject. The key to understanding this class of predicates is that the same predicate can be *said of* one subject and *in* another subject; it is not possible, however, that the same predicate is both *said of* and *in* the same subject. Take Aristotle's example of knowledge (1b1–2). Knowledge can be *in* a subject: this soul has knowledge. Predicating knowledge of the soul qualifies this soul; this predication describes a property of the soul, i.e. that it possesses knowledge. Knowledge can also be *said of* a subject: knowledge of grammar is knowledge. The term *knowledge* describes what kind of thing *knowledge of grammar* is, i.e. knowledge of grammar is a kind of knowledge. Note that in one case the subject is the soul and in the other case the subject is knowledge of grammar. This class of predicates that can be both *said of* and *in* a subject is more of a coincidence than a serious philosophical issue. It just so happens that some predicates can both be *said of* and *in* two different subjects.

We now arrive at the class of things that are neither *said of* nor *in* a subject; the things that fall under this class are not predicates at all. If there are only two ways of predicating, and this class satisfies neither, then it follows that this class is not a form of predication. This class is the foundation of Aristotle's ontology: 'A substance – that which is called a substance most strictly, primarily, and most of all – is that which is neither said of a subject nor in a subject, e.g. the individual man or the individual horse' (2a11–13). This is the class of subjects, i.e. things that can only be used as subjects and never as predicates. The kinds of things that can only serve as subjects are things that are individual and numerically one, e.g. this man, that horse, this tree, etc. These subjects are called *primary substances*, for without them none of the other forms of predication are possible: 'All the other things are either said of the primary substances as subjects or in them as subjects . . . So if the primary substances did not exist it would be impossible for any of the other things to exist'

(2b4–6). Aristotle continues: 'it is because the primary substances are subjects for all the other things and all the other things are predicated of them or are in them, that they are called substances most of all' (2b15–17). It is clear from the above that for Aristotle primary substances are primary precisely because they are the ultimate subjects of all predication. Without these subjects, there could be no predication. From this linguistic point, Aristotle reaches the following ontological conclusion: without primary substances, attributes and secondary substances would not exist.

Aristotle goes on to consider several characteristics of primary substance. I would like to draw attention to two of these characteristics in particular. First, Aristotle states, 'every substance seems to signify a certain "this"' (3b10). Aristotle means that a substance is a single thing. The contrary of a *this* in Aristotle's terminology is a *such-and-such*. While the former term reveals a single thing, the latter term reveals a class of things. Take as examples the individual Socrates and the species term *human being*. Socrates is a *this*; he is an individual thing that you can point to. The species term *human being* is a *such-and-such*; *human being* does not reveal a single thing, but rather a class of things, namely the class of human beings. Each human being is a *this*, but the class of human beings is a *such-and-such*. This characteristic of primary substance differentiates it from secondary substance. Here Aristotle indicates the difference between particular individual things and the universal terms used to classify such individuals. In ontological priority, a *this* is more of a substance than a *such-and-such*. Both in the *Categories* and in Aristotle's later treatments of substance, he always maintains that *this-ness* is a mark of substance. Things that are individual and numerically one are thus prior to universal terms.

A second key characteristic of substance is that 'what is numerically one and the same is able to receive contraries' (4a10–11). A primary substance is able to receive contraries and yet remain the same thing; this means that a primary substance persists through change.[5] Only primary substances exhibit this characteristic. Aristotle considers several examples to illustrate this point. A person can be pale at one time and dark at another; this person is thus able to receive contraries of colour and yet he remains the same person through this change. The colour white, on the other hand, cannot receive contraries and remain the same thing. If the colour white were to receive its contrary, i.e. the colour black, the colour white would no longer be white. It will have turned into a different thing; colours, then, do not persist through change. Aristotle states that qualities, qualifications and relations cannot persist through change; the ability to receive contraries and yet remain the same thing is a mark unique to primary substances.

We have thus reached the first major conclusions of Aristotle's investigation into being and substance. Let us now survey the philosophical consequences of Aristotle's ontology. In classifying the things that are said, Aristotle has revealed the ontological order of reality. Most basic to reality are primary substances; these are the individual members of species, e.g. this man or that horse. These are the entities upon which all else depends; were it not for these primary substances, Aristotle tells us, nothing else would exist. After the primary substances follow secondary substances, i.e. the species and genus terms. Of these, Aristotle tells us 'the species is more a substance than the genus, since it is nearer to primary substance. For if one is to say of the primary substance what it is, it will be more informative and apt to give the species than the genus' (2b8–10). Thus if we are classifying the primary substance Socrates, it is more informative to say that he is a human being than that he is an animal. To say of Socrates that he is a human being provides the most specific answer possible to the question, 'what kind of a thing is this?' Thus while it may sound odd to claim that 'the species is more a substance than the genus', Aristotle's reasoning does justify this claim. Both species and genus terms are real; that is why they are secondary substances, and as such, are a vital part of our ontology. What Aristotle is highlighting here is that species terms reveal the essential nature of a thing; genus terms accurately classify things, but they do not reveal the essential nature of a thing. This is why a species term is more of a substance than a genus term.

The final part of our ontology includes the quality, quantity and relation terms that are predicated of primary substances. Aristotle indicates that in being predicated of primary substances, these attributes that are *in* a subject are also predicated of secondary substances. If it is true that *Socrates is white*, then it is also true that *a human being is white* (3a1–5). Aristotle's ontology is thus clearly hierarchical. Primary substances are basic and foundational. Secondary substances reveal the essential nature of the primary substances, with the species term being more revealing, and thus more of a substance, than the genus term. Finally there are the qualification, quantification and relational terms. These terms are not substances; these terms exist only as attributes of substances. We have thus arrived at the basic framework of Aristotle's theory of substance. In what follows, I shall address some remaining issues and questions regarding Aristotle's theory.

One key issue that helps to illustrate the fundamental differences between Aristotle and Plato concerns the relationship of ontological dependence. Aristotle is clear that without primary substances none of the other things would exist; without the ultimate subjects, then, secondary substances and attributes would not exist (2b5–6). Things that are *said of* and *in* a subject thus depend for their existence upon primary substances. For Aristotle, if no human beings existed, then the universal term *human being* would not exist; the species term thus exists only because individual subjects who belong to the species actually exist. Likewise, if no bodies existed, then the universal term *white* would not exist; the quality of being coloured white can only exist if there exist bodies that are coloured white. This reasoning would apply for all species and genus terms as well as for all attributes. Aristotle's thesis regarding the ontological dependence of everything upon primary substance is most striking when compared with Plato's views.

We noted above that for Plato the Forms exist eternally. The Forms are immaterial and are not subject to change; truths about the Forms are thus eternal truths. Plato also maintains that the Forms would exist even if there were no particular material objects that instantiated the Forms; the Form of Beauty, for example, would exist and be knowable even if no beautiful things existed. Further, any existing beautiful things depend for their existence upon their participation in the Form of Beauty. The Forms are ontologically independent; the Forms do not depend on anything else for their existence, whereas everything else depends upon the Forms. The Forms are the most real and basic entities in Plato's ontology; particular material things are secondary and dependent. Let us consider how Plato and Aristotle would explain the existence of Socrates. For Plato, Socrates exists as a human being only because he participates in the Form of a human being; the Form of a human being would exist even if Socrates or any other human being did not exist. The Form of a human being is thus primary in Plato's ontological explanation; only by appeal to the Form of a human being can Plato explain the existence and nature of Socrates. For Aristotle, the explanation must begin with the individual subject Socrates. Socrates exists and depends upon nothing else for his existence; the species term *human being* only exists insofar as Socrates or some other human being exists. Were there no actually existing human beings, the species term *human being* would not exist. The relationships of ontological dependence in Plato and Aristotle are thus inverses of each other. For Plato, material subjects depend upon the immaterial Forms, whereas for Aristotle, the immaterial Forms depend upon the material subjects.

In general terms, we can thus say that both Plato and Aristotle accept the existence and reality of material subjects and immaterial universal terms, i.e. the Forms; they differ on the relationship of ontological dependence between the material subjects and the immaterial universal terms. For Aristotle, universal terms only exist if there is a scope for their application, i.e. if some actually existing material subject falls under the description of the universal term. Aristotle's view here is intuitive and aligns with common sense; after all, what does it mean to say that the universal term *human being* exists if there are no actually existing human beings? Surely we cannot meaningfully use the universal term *human being* unless we can point to an actually existing human being that is described by the universal term. The reality of the universal term *human being* thus depends upon the reality of an actual human being. As an illustrative thought experiment, we can envision a time in which human beings are extinct. At such a point, nothing would fall under the scope of the universal term *human being*. In a sense, the universal term *human being* would not be real because it does not describe any real existing thing. We can still think about the universal term *human being*; we can hold it in our minds as a concept. Existing in our minds as a concept, however, is not the same as existing as the classification of an actually existing thing. Only in the latter case can the universal term *human being* be properly described as a secondary substance.

The above discussion might suggest that aside from the inversion of the relationship of ontological dependence, Plato and Aristotle largely agree on basic matters of ontology. This is not quite true. First, the inversion of ontological dependence is no minor philosophical disagreement; their respective views on this point result in vastly different ontological schemes, though both schemes purport to explain the same reality. Second, there is a basic disagreement between Plato and Aristotle regarding what constitutes real and existing universal terms. Note how for Plato the universal terms that he calls Forms are abstract rational entities, e.g. Beauty, Justice, the Good, the Equal, etc. Now consider Aristotle's list of universal terms that he calls secondary substances: human being, horse, animal, oak, pine, plant, etc. Aristotle's universal terms are not abstract rational entities; rather, his key universal terms are species and genus terms that classify living entities. Aristotle's stance here leads to what we can call his *biological ontology*. For Aristotle, the most basic entities in reality, i.e. primary substances, are living individual things. The universal species and genus terms that classify these living individual things are secondary substances. The concept of life is thus central to Aristotle's ontology.

There are a number of ways in which Aristotle justifies this biological approach to ontology. For Aristotle, species are in a sense immortal; while the individual living members of a species die, the species itself lives on through the birth of new individual living things. This is how mortal things participate in immortality; insofar as mortal things are a part of an everlasting species, mortal things are part of something immortal.[6] Species terms also indicate a real distinction in the world. This is a crucial philosophical point. Aristotle derives this conclusion in part from the fact that species breed true to type; in Aristotle's often-repeated phrase, 'human begets human'. The fact that human beings do not give birth to horses or trees suggests to Aristotle that there is a real distinction between species. Aristotle's goal in the *Categories* is to classify the existing world. He does not want such a system of classification to be arbitrary, i.e. we divided up the world in this way but we just as well could have done it in any number of other ways. Aristotle's view is rather that there is one way to accurately classify reality. The correct way to classify must thus be based on real distinctions in reality. It has become common in philosophy to state that reality has joints or junctures, i.e. real distinctions between different kinds of things. Aristotle's secondary substances are thus an attempt to carve nature at the joints; using species and genus terms, Aristotle marks off different things from one another, separating them into natural kinds. Species and genus terms thus classify real and eternal parts of the world. This is why species and genus terms must be regarded as substance; they are not substance in the primary and strict sense, but they are the natural kinds into which primary substances fall.

Let us survey the explanatory power of Aristotle's biological ontology. If we are to begin our account of reality, according to Aristotle we must begin with primary substances. Our account could thus take the following form: in reality, there are things. These things are individual living members of species. These individual living things are substances most of all, and without these individual living things nothing else would exist. Individual living things fall into natural kinds; natural kinds are indicated by species and genus terms. In addition to falling into natural kinds, individual living things also have attributes. These attributes include qualities, quantities and relations. Completing our account of reality would thus involve describing and understanding the individual living things, the classes into which they fall and the attributes that they can possess.

Any account of reality should aspire to be complete and exhaustive, and we might wonder whether Aristotle has accomplished this. For example, we find around us numerous objects that are not individual living things. Human beings create artefacts, as do other living things. We build ships and houses, bees build hives and beavers build dams. Should we also consider such things as ships and houses primary substances even though they are not individual living things? In Aristotle's view, artefacts are not basic to our ontology; artefacts are accounted for when we explain the living things that construct such artefacts. Our account of human beings, then, will include an explanation of all the artefacts that human beings produce, just as our account of bees will include an explanation of their production of hives. Aristotle also argues that we can explain the features and properties of artefacts by appeal to the natural materials of which they are made. A bed, for example, is composed of wood and feathers. We need not admit beds into our ontology as a basic item, however; we can explain beds by appeal to the fact that humans construct them out of wood and feathers. The properties of the bed derive from the properties of the natural materials that compose the bed. Aristotle correctly observes that if we bury a wooden bed frame, if anything grows from it, it will not be a bed but a tree. Once again, we return to Aristotle's observation that 'human begets human'. A tree begets a tree, a bird begets a bird, but a bed does not beget a bed, nor does a ship beget a ship. These artefacts thus lack the crucial capacity for reproduction that is the mark of individual living things. Artefacts, then, are not basic to Aristotle's ontology; but his ontology is able to give a complete account of artefacts.

We can thus delineate the characteristics of primary substance: 1) primary substances are the subjects underlying all predication; 2) primary substances signify a 'this', i.e. individual and numerically one; 3) primary substances are able to receive contraries and remain the same thing; 4) primary substances fall into natural kinds, i.e. species and genus; 5) primary substances are able to beget new living entities of their species.

There remains one further point with respect to Aristotle's treatment of substance in the *Categories*. We may wonder whether Aristotle's theory of substance is unified; after all, there are two kinds of substance defended in the *Categories*. It seems that Aristotle is pulled in two different directions with regards to substance. Substance is regarded both as the thing that is, i.e. the individual subject, and what the thing is, i.e. the species and genus terms that classify the individual subject. In the *Categories*, Aristotle develops a theory of substance that answers two distinct questions. First, what is a thing? Second, what kinds of things are there? The former question is answered by appeal to the individual subject that is; the latter is answered by the universal species and genus terms.

Given that Aristotle is unwavering with respect to the ontological priority of primary substance, what reasons can we find for admitting species and genus terms as substance? We have already seen how, according to Aristotle, species and genus terms indicate real and eternal natural kinds into which living things fall. This is certainly one strong reason why Aristotle regards species and genus terms as (secondary) substance. Another compelling reason can be found through understanding Aristotle's connection to Plato. Aristotle largely accepts Plato's contention that scientific knowledge is knowledge about universal terms. Our scientific knowledge of human beings, for example, is formulated in terms of the species human being; we do not formulate our scientific knowledge in terms of the individual men Socrates or Callias. Scientific knowledge is stated in terms of generalizations about species and genus terms. Thus while universal species and genus terms depend upon individual subjects for their existence, scientific knowledge is based on universal terms. Because these universal terms are eternal and unchanging, universal terms are also more knowable than the individual subjects. The individual Socrates undergoes changes and eventually perishes; but, according to Aristotle, the species human being does not undergo such changes and will not perish. Any facts about Socrates will thus only be temporary and specific truths; facts about the species human being, however, will be eternal and general truths about all the individual subjects that have ever or will ever fall under the class of human beings. This justifies Aristotle's conclusion that the universals are more knowable than the individual subjects. In being more knowable, universal terms are thus better suited to the formulation of scientific knowledge. We thus see how even though Plato and Aristotle disagree on the ontological priority of universal terms, both accept the reality and knowability of universal terms.

While the above discussion helps to explain why species and genus terms are regarded as secondary substance, it remains unclear whether Aristotle's theory of substance is unified. We can see why he is pulled in two different directions in his theory of substance, but nevertheless he is pulled in two directions. We can note that Aristotle does attempt to unify his theory of substance. Consider the following:

> Further, it is because the primary substances are subjects for everything else that they are called substances most strictly. But as the primary substances stand to everything else, so the species and genera of the primary substances stand to all the rest: all the rest are predicated of these. For if you will call the individual person grammatical it follows that you will call both a person and an animal grammatical; and similarly in other cases. (3a1–6)

In this passage Aristotle demonstrates how both primary substances and secondary substances serve as subjects for predication. We are also presented with an analogy: as the primary substances stand to the other categories (including secondary substances), so do secondary substances stand to the rest of the categories (not including primary substance). When something is predicated of an individual person, that something is also predicated of the species and genus terms under which that person falls. Even though secondary substances are also predicates that are *said of* primary substances, here Aristotle emphasizes the role of secondary substances as subjects. They are not the ultimate subjects, to be sure; primary substances fill that role. Still, secondary substances are the penultimate subjects. In emphasizing the primary and secondary substances as the subjects of all predication, Aristotle makes some progress towards unifying his theory of substance in the *Categories*.

THE SCIENCE OF BEING: FIRST PHILOSOPHY

Aristotle's first significant treatment of being and substance is in the *Categories*, and this treatment is continued in several books of the *Metaphysics*. In the *Metaphysics*, Aristotle sets out to define the scope and content of a science of being; he calls this science *wisdom* or *first philosophy*. Before we venture into Aristotle's development of first philosophy, a few words about the *Metaphysics* are necessary. The *Metaphysics* is composed of 14 separate books varying in length and subject matter. These subjects range from the now familiar issues of substance and being as well as issues concerning the ultimate nature of reality, the nature of mathematics, and further issues concerning god and eternity that might be considered theology. Later editors assembled these books under the heading *metaphysics*; Aristotle himself did not organize these 14 books in this way, nor did he use the term *metaphysics* in his writings. A literal translation of the Greek word *metaphysics* is *after physics*; in the ancient catalogue of Aristotle's works, these 14 books were placed after Aristotle's *Physics*. The various subjects treated in Aristotle's *Metaphysics* helped to define the field of philosophy called metaphysics. Metaphysics has had a long history since its inception in these Aristotelian texts, and there is often disagreement about what is included in metaphysics and even whether metaphysics is at all worthwhile.

While it is an interesting historical accident that an entire field of philosophy takes its name from a seemingly insignificant editorial choice, it is important for our purposes to recognize that *metaphysics* is actually a misnomer for these 14 books; Aristotle likely would have resisted this title. The reason is simple: the issues treated in the *Metaphysics* do not come *after* anything else; these issues come *first*. The issues treated in the *Metaphysics* are prior to all other investigations and issues. We should note that the issues treated in the *Metaphysics* are not prior in a temporal sense; rather, they are prior in a logical and explanatory sense. Humans actually investigate these issues after other sciences have been investigated; but the issues in the *Metaphysics* are foundational for our scientific knowledge, and it is in this sense that they are prior to all other inquiries. It is thus more appropriate to use Aristotle's own phrases for this field of philosophy, i.e. *first philosophy*, *wisdom* or *theology*. Aristotle describes first philosophy as the first, the most authoritative and the most divine of all the sciences. In what follows, we will trace Aristotle's views about first philosophy, and in so doing, we will see how the treatment of substance and being in the *Categories* is enriched by the *Metaphysics*.

Before defining the scope and objects of first philosophy, Aristotle explains why humans pursue first philosophy at all. His answer illustrates his general conception of human beings and our relationship to knowledge. Consider the first line of the first book of the *Metaphysics*: 'all humans by nature desire to know' (980a20). Humans are a kind of animal, and just as other animals, we have desires. Desires are a function of our abilities to perceive and move. We share some of our desires with other animals; the desires for food and warmth, for example, are not unique to humans. The desire to know, however, is unique to us; for Aristotle, the desire to know is one of the main ways in which humans are distinguished from other kinds of animals. Knowledge satisfies a desire and brings us pleasure. We take delight in the senses, we derive pleasure from food and warmth, and knowing and understanding also bring us pleasure. We are the kind of animal that wonders and desires to know and understand. Consider this in connection to the following passage:

> For it is owing to their wonder that humans both now and at first began to philosophize; they wondered originally at the obvious difficulties, then advanced little by little and stated difficulties about the greater matters, e.g. about the phenomena of the moon and those of the sun and the stars, and about the genesis of the universe . . . since they philosophized in order to escape from ignorance, evidently they were pursuing science in order to know and not for any utilitarian end. And this is confirmed by the facts; for it was when almost all the necessities of life and the things that make for comfort and recreation were present that such knowledge began to be sought. Evidently, then, we do not seek it for any other advantage; but as the man is free, we say, who exists for himself and no other, so we pursue this as the only free science, for it alone exists for itself. (982b11–27)

In this passage, Aristotle argues that the history of early philosophy and science are evidence of the human desire to know. Aristotle also claims that humans began wondering and inquiring into first philosophy *simply to know*. While knowledge satisfies human desire, sometimes we seek knowledge for a specific utility; for example, we seek knowledge of architecture in order that we might construct beautiful and stable structures. First philosophy, however, is not pursued for any utilitarian end; it is pursued simply that we may escape from ignorance. Aristotle notes that in human history, humans pursued first philosophy only after our basic needs were met. First philosophy is thus not first in the order of discovery; rather, it is the science we arrive at last. First philosophy is first because it is the most general science of existing things. Because first philosophy is not pursued for any utility, it is a theoretical science. The goal of first philosophy is to know for the sake of knowing.

We know that first philosophy is pursued for its own sake; in this respect first philosophy is like the other theoretical sciences, i.e. mathematics and the natural sciences. The defining characteristic of theoretical sciences is that they aim only at understanding; theoretical sciences do not aim at action or production. The history of philosophy shows that 'all people suppose that what is called wisdom deals with the first causes and principles of things' (981b28). Note that Aristotle uses *causes* more broadly than our modern conception; for Aristotle, a cause is an explanation or a reason why something is the case. When we investigate first causes and principles of things, we investigate the ultimate explanations and origins of things. These first causes and principles are the *most universal* of the things that can be studied (982a24). The universality of first philosophy makes it the most difficult to study because its object is furthest from the senses; the senses perceive particulars, and as we get to greater and greater levels of universality, we move further and further from the senses. The science of first causes and principles is also the *most exact* of the sciences because it deals with the fewest number of principles. First philosophy is able to achieve a precision and exactness that derives from its limited number of principles. First philosophy is the *most knowable* of the sciences 'for by reason of these [the first causes and principles of first philosophy], and from these, all other things are known, but these are not known by means of the things subordinate to them' (982b1–4). For Aristotle, *most knowable* does not mean the easiest to know; we have seen already that first philosophy is the most difficult science to study owing to its universality. Rather, first philosophy is *most knowable* because it studies truths that are furthest from the senses. It is thus the *least sensible* science, and hence the *most knowable*.

We have thus arrived at a list of superlatives that characterize first philosophy: it is first among all sciences; it is the most universal, the most exact and the most knowable. We must add another superlative to this list: first philosophy is also the *most authoritative* of the sciences. Consider:

> And the science that knows to what end each thing must be done is the most authoritative of the sciences, and more authoritative than any ancillary science; and this end is the good in each class, and in general the supreme good in the whole of nature. (982b5–8)

In addition to studying first causes and principles, first philosophy studies ends or goals (*teloi*). For Aristotle, every activity or process in nature is directed at some end or goal. Nature is not merely accidental or mechanical; nature for Aristotle is directed at ends or goals. This contention is the main thesis of Aristotle's teleology.[7] The science that explains what are the ends for each thing is more authoritative than any other science. First philosophy studies the ends of each thing in the most general context possible, i.e. the supreme good in the whole of nature. Biology, for example, studies the ends of biological entities with respect to what is good for biological entities. Biology does not study the supreme good of nature; its range is more specific. Only first philosophy studies the ends of things in the context of the supreme good in the whole of nature, and for this reason, it is the most authoritative science. Another way to understand this point is to recognize that there is no science higher than first philosophy; the most authoritative science is the ultimate authority; there is no higher or further science to consult.

Aristotle adds a final superlative to his characterization of first philosophy: it is the *most divine* of the sciences. Aristotle acknowledges that the possession of first philosophy might be beyond human powers of reason; human nature and human reason are limited, and we might wonder whether it is possible for human beings to acquire this knowledge of first philosophy. It is reasonable to think that first philosophy might transcend human limitations, Aristotle claims, because first philosophy is in two senses the most divine science. First, it is divine because it is the science that would be most appropriate for god to have (983a6). Given that this science is the most authoritative, it would be impossible that god would lack knowledge of first philosophy. Second, first philosophy is divine because it deals with divine objects (983a6–7). God is a divine object, as are the heavenly bodies, in Aristotle's view; first philosophy is the science of such divine objects. God is thought to be a first cause or principle, and so first philosophy must study god. Other sciences study perishable objects; for example, biology studies perishable biological entities. In this latter respect, first philosophy seems to cover what we might call theological studies, i.e. the study of god and of divine entities.

Aristotle thus establishes an extraordinary list of superlatives that characterize first philosophy: most universal, most exact, most knowable, most authoritative, and most divine. This list is derived from *Metaphysics Alpha (1)*. Given this characterization, Aristotle seems justified in his conclusion that no science is better than first philosophy (983a10). While *Metaphysics Alpha* presents this inspiring description of first philosophy, we still do not know precisely how first philosophy proceeds in its investigations. It is this latter issue that is undertaken in *Metaphysics Gamma (4)*. *Metaphysics Gamma* marks the beginning of the philosophical project; the earlier books of the *Metaphysics* are largely introductory and preliminary. It is in *Metaphysics Gamma* that Aristotle makes some progress in first philosophy. All sciences investigate some specific and definite object; the first task of *Metaphysics Gamma* is to define the specific object of first philosophy. Second, Aristotle defends the principles or axioms of first philosophy. By the conclusion of *Metaphysics Gamma*, we will have arrived at a more concrete understanding of what first philosophy investigates and how its investigations proceed.

The first line of *Metaphysics Gamma* describes the object of first philosophy: 'there is a discipline that studies being *qua* being and those things that hold good of this in its own right' (1003a21–22). First philosophy thus studies being *qua* being. At first glance this phrase might seem mysterious. What does it mean to study being *qua* being, or in an alternate translation, that which is *qua* thing-that-is? There are several possible translations for the Latin word *qua*: *insofar as, considered as*, or *as*. For clarity and brevity, we can use the latter translation: being *as* being. To study being as being means that we study the things that are; but we study the things that are only insofar as they are things that are. First philosophy thus investigates the things that are and it seeks to explain what is true of the things that are simply in virtue of the fact that they exist. First philosophy thus studies existence or being in general. This generality of first philosophy is perhaps best illustrated through example. All sciences study things that are; there is no science of non-existing things. But each of the sciences studies things that are in a special way: biology studies the things that are insofar as these things are living things; mathematics and geometry study the things that are insofar as these things exhibit number and figure; chemistry studies the things that are insofar as these things are composed of chemicals; and so on. Each of these disciplines carves off a specific aspect of existing things and studies that aspect. First philosophy does not study any specific aspect of existing things; instead, it studies the most general aspect of existing things, namely, that which is true of existing things simply in virtue of the fact that they exist.

Aristotle further clarifies this object of first philosophy with a discussion of the verb *is*. Aristotle first notes, 'that which *is* may be so called in various ways' (1003a32). There are several ways in which we use this verb. We can use this verb to predicate an attribute of a substance, e.g. Socrates is pale. While there may be several uses of this verb, Aristotle argues that all the various uses of *is* refer to the one original sense of *is*, which is existence. First philosophy studies this original sense of *is*. First philosophy thus studies that which *simply is*, rather than that which *is something*. First philosophy studies statements of the following form: Socrates is, god is, etc. First philosophy does not study statements that predicate something other than existence. This focus on the original sense of *is* aligns with Aristotle's claim that first philosophy seeks 'origins, i.e. the most extreme causes' (1003a22). First philosophy will make clear what is true of the things that are as things-that-are: 'certain things are distinctive of that which is *qua* thing-that-is, and these are the things about which it falls to the philosopher to investigate the truth' (1004b15–16).

Given that existing things are substances, 'the philosopher will need to have the principles and causes of substances' (1003b18). We thus have arrived at a clear description of the proper object of first philosophy: first philosophy studies substances as substances, being as being; first philosophy attempts to determine what is true of substances as substances; first philosophy also seeks to understand the causes and principles of substance. Thus we see how Aristotle's concern with substance in the *Categories* is now developed into a systematic science of substance.

First philosophy must thus study substance and the things that hold good of substance. Aristotle provides a list of concepts that it falls to the philosopher to explain. Every thing-that-is is one thing. This is a general truth about substances; no matter what kind of thing we are concerned with, each thing is one thing. This might seem like a trivial observation, but this observation gives rise to the concept of unity, which it falls to the philosopher to make intelligible. If we explain unity, we must also explain its contrary, i.e. plurality. How things are one and how they are many thus fall under the scope of first philosophy. The concepts of sameness and difference are also the domain of first philosophy. Note the general nature of each of these concepts. These concepts are not specific to any particular field of study; rather these concepts apply to every possible field of study. This further justifies Aristotle's claim that first philosophy is the most universal of the sciences; it studies substance and the things that hold true of substance in the most general way possible. What is true of substance in first philosophy will hold good in whatever scientific discipline we pursue; this is what Aristotle means when he states that all other sciences are subordinate to first philosophy. The concepts of unity, plurality, sameness and difference will be treated by first philosophy; that treatment will apply to all other sciences. Biology does not have its own concept of unity while chemistry has another. Rather, it is the same concept of unity explained by first philosophy that is used in every other science.

All of the sciences are demonstrative or axiomatic; as we saw above, Aristotle applies the geometrical model of axioms to all scientific knowledge. First philosophy will thus have axioms. Aristotle claims that the philosopher should be able to state the firmest principles or axioms of his or her subject. Given that our subject is first philosophy, the firmest principle of this subject will be the firmest principle of everything (1005b10–11). All else is subordinate to first philosophy, so the firmest principle of first philosophy will be the firmest principle of all; all other sciences and the principles of those sciences will fall under the scope of this firmest principle of first philosophy. Aristotle states this principle: 'For the same thing to hold good and not to hold good simultaneously of the same thing and in the same respect is impossible' (1005b19–20). This is commonly known as the law of non-contradiction, and Aristotle claims that it is impossible to be in error about this principle. In simplest terms, this law states that no contradiction can be true. Consider the individual Socrates. If Socrates' skin is pale, it is not possible that at the same time and in the same respect his skin is also not pale. At some other time or in some other respect it is possible that his skin is not pale; but this is not possible at the same time and in the same respect that he is pale. There is a further psychological law that is derived from this law of non-contradiction; Aristotle holds that it is impossible for a person to believe that the same thing holds good and does not hold good of the same thing, at the same time and in the same respect (1005b30).

Aristotle makes several important points about this firmest of all principles. First, this principle is not a hypothetical principle; this principle is actually used by all and it is a necessary part of any scientific understanding (1005b15). Second, this principle cannot be demonstrated (1006a6–8). As we have seen already, the principles of a science cannot be demonstrated; principles are known through intuition but not through demonstration. Demonstrations can only occur by appeal to principles that are higher and firmer than that being demonstrated; but since there is no principle higher or firmer than the law of non-contradiction, there is nothing to which to appeal in order to demonstrate this principle. Finally, Aristotle argues that it is only by accepting the law of non-contradiction that we are able to have anything definite in our thinking (1009a4–5). Without this law, we could not signify or act. When we utter the word *human*, for example, we are signifying something by this word, and we are signifying that *human* is different from *not-human*. If one could not distinguish between things in this way, 'there will be nothing for such a person to speak or say; for he simultaneously says this and not this. And if a person believes nothing, but considers it equally so and not so, how would his or her state be different from a vegetable's?' (1008b10–11). Rational thought and speech depend upon the law of non-contradiction.

We have thus developed an understanding of the science of being as well as the first principle of this science. Aristotle has discussed the object of this science as well as where this science fits in the overall structure of scientific knowledge. The project of completing this science may be daunting, but it is at least conceivable that we could complete it. Aristotle has basically provided a research programme for first philosophy; it remains for the philosophers who follow him to complete the investigations he has begun. Aristotle has not, however, given his final thoughts on this science of being. In the following section, we will survey one of Aristotle's most perplexing and difficult texts on substance, i.e. *Metaphysics Zeta (7)*; this text is absolutely crucial for furthering this inquiry into substance.

BEING IN *METAPHYSICS ZETA (7)*

We began this inquiry into substance with the general question *what is being* or *what is substance*. Through the *Categories* and *Metaphysics Alpha* and *Gamma*, we have now arrived at an answer to this question. Substances are individual living members of species. These are what we might call sensible substances, for they are substances that we can perceive with our senses. We also learned that the science of substance studies divine objects; divine objects are thus another kind of substance. God and the heavenly spheres are not sensible substances, but they are substances nonetheless. While Aristotle has answered the question *what is substance*, in *Metaphysics Zeta* he considers what it is that makes a substance a substance. In other words, he investigates what explains the substance of a thing. Recall that for Aristotle a cause is understood as an explanation or a reason. When we explain the causes and principles of substance, then, we need to make intelligible what about substances makes them substances.

Aristotle offers some preliminary remarks about substance; many of these remarks echo points he has already made. He repeats his claim that it is substance that underlies all the other categories, and that none of the other categories would exist without substance (1028a28). He also states that when we seek substance, we seek 'that which is primarily and *is* simply (not is something)' (1028a29–30). We are thus investigating the original sense of *is*, i.e. existence. Further, Aristotle states, 'substance is primary in every sense – in formula, in order of knowledge, in time' (1028a32). Substance is primary in formula because in any formula (or definition) of a thing, the substance of the thing must be present. We cannot provide a formula for a thing without first making explicit the substance of a thing. Substance is primary in order of knowledge because 'we know each thing most fully when we know what it is', i.e. what its essential nature is (1028b1). Aristotle also states that separability and individuality belong to substance. By separability, Aristotle means that

substance is capable of being separated; substance is thus independent and needs nothing else for existence. Aristotle sometimes refers
to this feature of substance as self-subsistence; substance is complete
on its own; it needs nothing else to be the substance that it is. The
claim that individuality belongs to substance is another way of
claiming that a substance is a *this*, i.e. an individual and numerically
one thing. Notice that in these preliminary remarks substance has a
double meaning: substance is the individual and separable thing,
and substance is the essential nature of individual and separable
things. It is important to keep in mind this double meaning of *substance* throughout Aristotle's discussion in *Metaphysics Zeta*.

There are four main ways in which the word *substance* is used:
essence, universal, genus, and substratum (1028b34–35). This is
Aristotle's list of candidates for what explains the substance of a
thing. In the following, we will investigate each of these alternatives.
This method of proceeding is characteristic of Aristotle; he surveys
what has been said about substance. There are reasons why substance has been spoken of in these four ways; Aristotle endeavours
to determine whether these ways of speaking about substance lead
us into difficulty. We must also note a second methodological point;
Aristotle will investigate substance by looking for it among sensible
things (1029a34–1029b11). While god and the heavenly bodies are
also substances, these are more difficult for us to grasp. We must start
with that which is most intelligible to us. The sensible objects that
surround us are most intelligible to us. Aristotle distinguishes here
between what is intelligible *to us* and what is intelligible *by nature*.
What is intelligible *to us* is what is closest to our senses. But what is
closest to our senses are not the most intelligible things by nature;
what is most intelligible *by nature* is that which is most knowable, i.e.
that about which we can arrive at the most exact truths. God and the
heavenly spheres are thus the most knowable and intelligible things
by nature; but we must start our inquiry into substance with what is
intelligible to us. Once we are clear on the latter, we can turn to the
former.

Let us now turn to Aristotle's candidates for what explains the
substance of a thing. He treats the substratum first. The substratum
is conceived as the underlying thing: 'the substratum is that of which
other things are predicated, while it is not itself predicated of anything else' (1028b36). This is a now familiar characteristic of substance. The substratum is spoken of in three distinct ways, so in

considering substratum as a candidate for the substance of a thing, Aristotle considers the substratum as *matter, form* and the *compound* of matter and form. This analysis of things in terms of matter, form and the compound of the two is a central component of Aristotle's philosophical approach; it is thus vital to be clear on the meaning of these terms.

Anything that exists can be analysed in terms of its matter and form. Aristotle employs the example of a bronze statue. The matter of the statue is the bronze, i.e. the material of which the statue is composed. But the statue is not just bronze; it is bronze arranged in a certain way; it has a certain shape or plan. This is the form of a thing. Note that this conception of form is crucially different from Plato's theory of the Forms. Aristotle's forms are embodied in a thing; there are specifically not disembodied immaterial forms. Aristotle's forms are the shape and plan that matter takes in order to be anything at all; on Aristotle's account, it makes no sense to speak of forms existing without matter. The compound of matter and form is just the individual thing, i.e. the bronze statue. There is, however, some overlap between Aristotle's account of form and Plato's. Aristotle generally uses two terms to describe form: *morphe* and *idea*. *Morphe* corresponds to the sensible shape of a thing, while *idea* corresponds to the intelligible idea of a thing. Plato refers to form exclusively in the latter sense of intelligible idea. For Aristotle, form includes both the sensible shape of a thing and the intelligible idea of a thing. When we conceive of the form of a substance, then, we must attend to the sensible shape of the substance as well as the intelligible idea or plan of the substance. It is important to note that breaking down a thing in terms of matter and form is a theoretical and logical exercise. It is not the case that we ever find in the world matter without form, or form without matter. Even a pile of dirt has the form of a pile; formless matter is a theoretical concept, just as immaterial form is a theoretical concept. In the world, all we find are the compounds of matter and form, i.e. the individual and numerically one substances. The compound of matter and form results in the unity that is an individual thing.

While we never encounter matter and form separately, Aristotle argues that it is fruitful to analyse entities in terms of their material and formal elements. When we are confronted with a thing, it is sensible to ask whether the form or the matter of the thing makes it the thing it is. Aristotle immediately rules out the compound of matter and form as explaining the substance of a thing: 'the substance compounded of both matter and form may be dismissed, for it is posterior and its nature is obvious' (1029a30). Substance is primary in every sense; the compound of matter and form, however, is posterior, for in order of explanation it comes after matter and form.

Aristotle next considers whether the matter of a thing is adequate to explain its substance. If we accept the notion that substance is that of which all else is predicated, it seems that matter becomes substance: 'For if this [matter] is not substance, it is beyond us to say what else is. When all else is taken away evidently nothing but matter remains' (1029a10–11). When we take away all attributes, such as colour, length and relation, it seems that all that is left is the underlying matter. For example, if we take the individual Socrates and strip him of all attributes, nothing remains but the matter. Once we have taken away his paleness, the snubness of his nose, his height and mass, there is nothing left but the matter that composed Socrates. Aristotle clarifies this conception in his definition of matter: 'By matter I mean that which in itself is neither a particular thing nor of a certain quantity nor assigned to any of the other categories by which being is determined' (1029a20–21). Here Aristotle is considering matter as undifferentiated stuff; matter here is not a particular thing, nor is it characterized by any of the categories of being. Conceive if you can of matter without qualities, quantities or relations. Aristotle asks if matter in this sense explains the substance of a thing.

Aristotle concludes that it is impossible for matter to be substance because 'both separability and individuality are thought to belong chiefly to substance' (1029a27–28). Matter is not an individual *this*; matter is not a thing. Aristotle thus clearly has in mind a conception of substance as an individual thing; we have seen evidence of this conception since the account of primary substance in the *Categories*. Bare matter is undifferentiated stuff; bare matter is not a separable and individual thing. Matter is certainly required for anything to exist, but it is not the matter that makes something what it is. The same stones and wood, for example, could be shaped to make a house or a pile of rubble; the same blood and flesh could be part of any number of different kinds of animals. The matter is a necessary component of anything, but it does not explain why the thing is the thing it is. Of the three senses of the substratum, matter and the compound of matter and form have been ruled out; only form remains as a viable candidate.

We can consider the force of Aristotle's arguments regarding matter against the views of the Presocratic philosophers. The Presocratics held that the *arche* or first principle of nature could be found either in material stuffs, e.g. water, air, fire and earth, or in atoms. Aristotle here contends that such material stuffs do not suffice as the first principle of nature; these material stuffs are not sufficient to explain substance. The fact that matter is not a *this* is for Aristotle a decisive point; *this-ness* is thought to belong primarily to substance. The Presocratics may have explained an aspect of the substratum, namely that it has a material component, but this aspect does not adequately explain substance or being. For Aristotle, the substance of a thing must explain what makes that thing the definite thing that it is.

Much of the remaining material in *Metaphysics Zeta* defends the view that it is the form or essence of a thing that explains its being. Aristotle says, 'the essence of each thing is what it is said to be in virtue of itself' (1029b13). Aristotle attempts a new approach to the question of substance, here emphasizing the explanatory role of substance:

> Thus the inquiry [into substance] is about the predication of one thing of another. And why are certain things, i.e. stones and bricks, a house? Plainly we are seeking the cause. And this is the essence (to speak abstractly). (1041a25–29)

It is the form or essence that is a principle and a cause or explanation. When we ask why these stones and bricks form this house and not something else, it is the presence of the essence of a house that answers this question: 'Therefore what we seek is the cause, i.e. the form, by reason of which the matter is some definite thing; and this is the substance of the thing' (1041b8–9). The form or essence is not merely the sensible shape of a thing. When we seek an explanation of why these bricks and stones form a house, the answer is not only that they are shaped like a house. The answer must also include that the house is designed and constructed for shelter; the essence of a house is the fact that it is used for shelter by human beings. Stones and bricks may be arranged to look like a house, but if they cannot adequately shelter human beings, then the essence of a house is not present. The sensible shape is thus part of the form or essence, but it is not the entirety of form or essence. Recall that for Aristotle form includes both the sensible shape (*morphe*) and the intelligible idea (*idea*).

Aristotle continues by explaining that form or essence is not an element. Essence is not a part of a thing; rather, essence is a principle of a thing. Consider this line of reasoning from Aristotle:

> The syllable is not its elements, *ba* is not the same as *b* and *a*, nor is flesh fire and earth; for when they are dissolved the wholes, i.e. the flesh and the syllable, no longer exist, but the elements of the syllable exist, and so do fire and earth. The syllable, then, is something – not only its elements (the vowel and the consonant) but also something else; and the flesh is not only fire and earth or the hot and the cold, but also something else. But it would seem that this is something, and not an element, and that it is the cause which makes *this* thing flesh and *that* a syllable . . . And this is the substance of each thing; for this is the primary cause of its being. (1041b13–19, 25–29)

Aristotle tells us that essence is not related to a thing as an element is related to a thing. A thing can be broken down into its constituent elements, but essence is not one of these elements. With this point we see Aristotle once again differentiating his views from the materialist views of the Presocratics; for the Presocratics, substance is an element. Nor is essence or form an immaterial Platonic Form. The substance of a thing is explained by the principle of structure in a concrete thing; this is done by the form or essence. Crucially, this form or essence is embodied in the concrete individual thing; it is not a disembodied Platonic Form.

Consider how this approach would explain the substance of Socrates. What makes this collection of blood and tissue Socrates rather than some other thing? The essence of Socrates is present. This does not only mean that the blood and tissue are shaped to look like Socrates. It also means that the principle of organization and structure that makes Socrates Socrates is present. Aristotle's view here has considerable intuitive appeal. It is surely inadequate to explain the nature of a thing only by appeal to its matter; it is the presence of matter organized and structured in a particular way. There is something more than simply an aggregation of elements present in a thing. There is the presence of form or essence, and this is what we have been seeking in substance all along.

In addition to establishing form or essence as the substance of a thing, *Metaphysics Zeta* also further differentiates Aristotle's conception of form or essence from the Platonic Forms. In Chapters 13–16 of *Metaphysics Zeta*, Aristotle considers and rejects the possibility of Forms or universals as substance. There are two main points that lead to Aristotle's rejection of the Forms. Consider first the following:

> It seems impossible that any universal term should be the name of a substance. For primary substance is that kind of substance which is peculiar to an individual, which does not belong to anything else; but the universal is common, since that which is called universal naturally belongs to more than one thing. (1038b8–11)

In this passage Aristotle advances the view that primary substance is unique or peculiar to a thing; common or universal terms cannot satisfy this criterion. Let us call this criterion the Peculiarity Requirement. The Platonic Forms are common terms, and so they cannot be primary substance. For example, it is the same Form *human being* that explains the nature of each existing human being; each human being is a human being because of his or her participation in the same universal Form *human being*.

The Peculiarity Requirement rules out the possibility that Platonic Forms could be primary substance, but this requirement also raises difficulties for Aristotle's own view. Aristotle has argued that it is the embodied form or essence that explains the substance of a thing. But according to the Peculiarity Requirement, the embodied form or essence must be unique and peculiar to a thing. If the embodied form or essence were a common term, then it would run afoul of the Peculiarity Requirement in the same way as the Platonic Forms. I suggest the following as a way for Aristotle to preserve the Peculiarity Requirement and defend his view regarding embodied form or essence. Consider two men, Socrates and Callias. Both of these men are human beings, and so their embodied form or essence is the form of a human being. But now we must ask, is the embodied form or essence of Socrates identical to the embodied form or essence of Callias? I suggest that the embodied forms are identical in all respects but one: one of the forms is embodied in Socrates, while the other is embodied in Callias. In every other respect these forms are identical; these forms provide the same plan, shape and structure for the substances. *Qua* the form of a human being, these forms are identical. But these forms are the forms of different human beings, and so they are not identical. This means that the form of Socrates is peculiar to Socrates; it is found nowhere else but in Socrates. We have thus reconciled the Peculiarity Requirement with Aristotle's view that the embodied form or essence explains the substance of a thing.

As a second reason for rejecting Platonic Forms as primary substance, Aristotle notes that universal terms function as subjects as well as predicates. One can state, for example, *a human being is pale* and *Socrates is a human being*; in the latter, the universal is a predicate while in the former the universal is a subject. The universal term *human being* is always predicable of some subject, namely any existing individual human being. Against this, Aristotle claims, 'substance means that which is not predicable of a subject, but the universal is predicable of some subject always' (1038b15). Here Aristotle contends that substance in the primary sense is that which is the ultimate subject and never a predicate; because universals are predicates they cannot be substance in the primary sense. This view largely coheres with Aristotle's view in the *Categories*, where he concluded that universals are substance in a secondary sense. This secondary sense of substance explains what kind of a thing something is, but it does not uniquely explain what makes something the thing it is. It is this latter point that Aristotle seeks to satisfy with his conception of embodied form or essence as the substance of a thing.

It should be noted, however, that the same tension present in Aristotle's theory of substance in the *Categories* is also present in *Metaphysics Zeta*. While Aristotle never wavers from his contention that individual subjects are substances most of all, he also contends that scientific knowledge is about universal terms. We study individual subjects such as human beings, but our knowledge is stated as being about the universal species term *human being*. Socrates and *Callias* are not terms found in biology; terms such as *human being* and *tree* are found in biology. In Aristotle's terms, an item of scientific knowledge must be knowable and definable; only universals can be truly known and defined. Particular subjects are neither fully knowable nor definable. Many of the most difficult and puzzling passages in *Metaphysics Zeta* are an attempt to resolve this tension. While it is beyond our scope to follow Aristotle's tortuous line of reasoning on this issue, it is at least apparent what the tension is and why it arises for Aristotle. His account of substance is torn between the most real things and the most knowable things. Alternative onto-logical views, such as Plato's, do not suffer from this same tension; for Plato, the most knowable things and the most real things are the same thing, i.e. the Forms.

We have thus traced Aristotle's inquiry into substance through the *Categories* and several books of the *Metaphysics*. His general view has become clear. In nature, those things that are substances most of all are individual members of species. These individual and numer-ically one substances are the ultimate subjects for all predication; universal species and genus terms as well as attributes would not exist without these individual substances. Species and genus terms as well as attributes are not self-subsistent in the way that substances are. Species and genus terms do not indicate a *this*, which is the mark of substance; rather, species and genus terms indicate a *such-and-such*. Separability and individuality thus belong to substance. Aristotle's theory of substance also explains what it is about an indi-vidual thing that explains its substance. It is the embodied form or essence, which is a principle of structure and organization, that explains what makes anything the thing it is. In developing his theory of substance, Aristotle offers compelling reasons why the Presocratic materialist approach and the Platonic immaterialist approach are unsatisfactory accounts of substance. Aristotle also develops a science of substance, which he calls first philosophy. First philosophy is at the top of Aristotle's hierarchy of scientific knowl-edge; in studying substance, i.e. being *qua* being, first philosophy studies truths that apply to all the specific scientific disciplines. We have thus seen Aristotle's account of substance as well as the place of his science of substance in the body of human knowledge.

CHAPTER 3

NATURE (*PHUSIS*)

We now move from the general science of substance to the science of natural substances; we move from first philosophy to second philosophy. Our primary text for second philosophy is found in the first two books of the *Physics*. That title is somewhat misleading, for as we read through Aristotle's *Physics* we find little that resembles physics, as we know it. The Greek title for this text is *phusis*, which means simply *nature*. The term *physics* is thus a transliteration rather than an accurate translation of *phusis*. Keeping this in mind, it is more appropriate to use the following labels for this discipline: second philosophy, philosophy of nature, or natural science. Each of these labels provides a more accurate description of the issues under discussion in the *Physics*; in using these labels, we will also avoid the unhelpful connotations of *physics* as a description of Aristotle's work. In this chapter, we will examine Aristotle's definition of nature; what nature is and what kinds of things have a nature are the first issues we must settle. We will also examine his argument for the principles or axioms of second philosophy. We have already seen Aristotle's conception of demonstrative or axiomatic science; in his philosophy of nature, we see him develop the first principles or axioms of natural science. Aristotle also presents his famous doctrine of the four causes in the *Physics*; this is a doctrine central to Aristotle's thought. By understanding this doctrine, we will establish a clear idea of what the natural scientist must explain. Finally, we will conclude our treatment of Aristotle's philosophy of nature with his defence of teleology. Aristotle contends that everything in nature is for something, i.e. everything in nature has goals or ends (*teloi*); in *Physics* 2.8 Aristotle gives his most compelling defence of the reality of ends in nature. We will thus investigate what nature is, what the principles of natural science are, what kinds of causes natural science must explain, and finally, why everything in nature is directed at some end.

We have already noted that for Aristotle nature is the sublunary realm, i.e. the realm below the orbit of the earth's moon. For Aristotle the extralunary realm, i.e. the place beyond the orbit of the earth's moon, is a realm of eternal and unchanging objects. The heavenly bodies have always been and will always be. The heavenly bodies also move differently than objects on earth. Heavenly bodies move unceasingly in circles. Because the heavens are the realm of unchanging objects in unceasing circular motion, Aristotle posited that the heavens were composed of a fifth element not found on earth, i.e. the ether. The sublunary realm, by contrast, is the realm of perishable objects that are subject to change. These objects do not naturally move in circular motion; rather, they move up and down; their motion is rectilinear. The sublunary realm is composed of the four standard elements: earth, air, water and fire. While we now recognize that Aristotle's distinction between the sublunary and the extralunary is false, we can at least identify the reasoning that led him to such a distinction. For Aristotle, natural science and astronomy were fundamentally distinct fields studying different kinds of objects; we have, however, corrected this mistake and now include astronomy as a natural science.

Aristotle begins Book 2 of the *Physics* by providing a definition of nature. He considers several objects that all would agree are due to nature, e.g. animals, plants and the simple elements like earth, air, water and fire. Consider:

> All the things mentioned [natural objects] plainly differ from things which are *not* constituted by nature. For each of them has within itself a principle of motion and stationariness (in respect of place, or of growth and decrease, or by way of alteration) (192b14–15).[1]

The main kinds of changes that natural objects undergo include growth and decay as well as movement. The growth and decay of a natural object is dictated by something internal to the object; a natural object's plan for growth and decay is in a sense already written in the object. This internal source of change is part of the plan of a natural object; a natural object will go through growth and decay in stages according to the internal source of change in the natural object.

By contrast, Aristotle continues, artefacts do not contain in themselves a source of change or staying unchanged. Consider a wooden bed frame. A wooden bed frame undergoes changes, but it undergoes changes not as a bed frame, but as something composed of wood. The properties of the bed frame can be understood with reference to the natural bodies that compose the bed frame, namely wood. Aristotle also notes that if a wooden bed frame is buried, anything that sprouts from it will be a tree and not a bed (193b10). This provides a clear distinction between natural objects and artefacts: natural objects have within them a source of change, while artefacts undergo change insofar as they are composed of natural bodies. We can recall Aristotle's claim that a human being begets a human being, while a bed does not beget a bed. Contrast this example of an artefact with a natural object. A tree, for example, changes as a tree does; it has a tree's nature. It grows and decays; it sprouts upward and shoots branches outward. A tree does all these things as a tree. Further, all of these changes are intrinsic to the tree. We do not need to invoke any other substances in order to explain the tree; a tree is self-subsistent and separable. A bed, however, can only be explained by appeal to a substance, namely the tree out of which the bed is composed. Any changes that the tree undergoes it undergoes *qua* tree, while the bed undergoes changes not *qua* bed, but *qua* something composed of natural bodies. Anything that has such an internal source of change has a nature (192b33).[2]

Aristotle next considers whether matter or form is more properly identified as constituting the nature of a thing. We can recall the discussions from *Metaphysics Zeta* regarding whether matter or form explain the substance of a thing. There Aristotle concluded that it was form or essence that explained the substance of a thing. Here in the *Physics*, Aristotle also settles on form rather than matter as constituting the essential nature of a thing. He reasons that the matter of a natural substance cannot fully explain the tendency to movement, growth and decay. Matter, Aristotle argues, is only possibility. The matter alone does not determine what a thing actually is; matter alone only determines what a thing possibly could be. But, Aristotle continues, we say that something has a nature when it is actualized and not merely possible. This means that something has a nature when the form is present. Consider the following example of flesh and bone: 'What is potentially flesh or bone has not yet its own nature, and does not exist by nature, until it receives the form specified in the definition, which we name in defining what flesh or bone is' (193b1–3). The matter that is only possibly flesh and bone does not yet constitute a natural thing; once form is present, the matter is actualized as part of a natural thing. The matter that was only possibly flesh and bone is now actually the flesh and bone of some living organism. Thus it is the form of a natural thing that best explains its nature.

Aristotle appeals to a second argument in order to establish form as the nature of a thing. We have seen already how Aristotle rejects a purely mechanistic account of the world as proposed by the Presocratic philosophers. Here in the *Physics* we also see his rejection of mechanism. Matter alone could not completely explain the behaviours of natural things; this is because the behaviours of natural things are not due only to their matter. For Aristotle, everything in nature, and particularly living things, pursues goals. The form of a thing also explains the ends or goals (*teloi*) of a natural object. We shall discuss Aristotle's teleology more fully in the last two sections of this chapter. For here, let it suffice to say that for Aristotle natural objects have goals; they seek certain ends. The key term for this notion is *the cause for the sake of which*; this term highlights the idea that an end is a reason why an organism engages in a particular behaviour. This aim also benefits the organism in some way. The matter of a thing cannot explain this goal-directed behaviour. Take, for example, a spider's construction of a web. This behaviour, according to Aristotle, is clearly goal-directed: through constructing the web, the spider seeks to capture its prey. In capturing prey, the spider benefits itself. How then do we explain this behaviour? Appealing to matter alone is not sufficient; the strictly mechanical explanation does not provide a complete understanding for why the spider engages in this behaviour. Mechanism can only explain material changes, but mechanism cannot explain why those changes occur, i.e. the goal that the spider achieves through its construction of a web. Rather, the behaviour is best explained as a goal-directed process, and the form of a thing accounts for this. It is the form of a thing, then, that explains the ends or goals of a thing. The argument concerning actuality and the argument concerning ends both lead Aristotle to conclude that in the primary sense the nature of a thing is its form.

Let us examine Aristotle's rejection of mechanism from another perspective. The mechanist treats the whole as the sum of its parts; the whole organism, then, is treated as being composed of its constitutive elements. An explanation of the organism would thus be in terms of its constituent elements, their size, shape and motion. But Aristotle argues against this that the student of nature must treat the parts in light of the whole. Certain parts, for example, only make sense in light of the overall goals of the organism. For Aristotle, the parts of animals cannot be properly understood in isolation; they make sense only in relation to the whole organism. The whole, for Aristotle, is more than just the sum of its parts. A thing is not just an aggregate of molecules; each thing is a whole that has goals for itself as a whole. This is why the student of nature treats form as primary. In understanding form, we understand the whole and can understand the parts with respect to the whole. The mechanist treats natural objects as nothing more than the sum of their parts; in doing so, they fail to recognize form and goals. The mechanist thus offers an incomplete account of nature. Aristotle's account of nature attempts to improve upon these shortcomings. This is not to suggest, however, that mechanical explanations are irrelevant to our study of nature. Aristotle explicitly includes the material as being part of the explanation of any natural process. Thus mechanism is not incorrect as a type of explanation; rather, it is incomplete. To understand a natural process, we must understand the matter and the form. This suggests that our mechanical explanations must be complemented by teleological and formal explanations. Aristotle's basic point is that explanations through form and ends reveal a real part of natural processes and substances that is not captured by strictly mechanical explanations.

While Aristotle clearly establishes the priority of form over matter, he steadfastly maintains that the matter must be a part of our study of nature. He contrasts this approach with the strictly mathematical approach of the Platonists. Mathematics studies number and figure in abstraction from physical bodies; the mathematician separates number and figure from physical bodies and studies only number and figure. Lost in this abstraction, according to Aristotle, are the matter and movement of a physical body. This is no great loss if our study is only mathematical; but if we are studying natural bodies, we cannot separate matter and movement from such bodies. The matter is integrally involved in physical bodies, and we cannot study physical bodies in abstraction from their matter. This is the key difference between mathematics and natural science. Thus while the nature of a thing is primarily its form, the student of nature must study nature both as form and as matter. This means that the student of nature must study matter insofar as it is required for the realization of form. For example, you cannot make blood and bone out of just any matter; to realize the form of a living thing, there are certain requirements for the matter. Consider Aristotle's remarks:

> [I]t is part of the same discipline to know the form and the matter up to a point (e.g. the doctor has a knowledge of health and also of bile and phlegm, in which health is realized and the builder both of the form of the house and of the matter, namely that which is bricks and beams, and so forth): if this is so, it would be the part of natural science also to know nature in both its senses [i.e. matter and form]. (194a21–26)

The student of nature must thus study the matter *up to a point*. The builder must know what kind of matter is required to realize the form of a house. The doctor must know how the form of health is realized in the matter of bodily fluids. There is simply no way to understand these natural objects by attending only to form; the student of nature must know the matter as well. Both the mechanist and the mathematician thus offer incomplete accounts of nature. We have now seen how, according to Aristotle, each of their accounts falls short.

We can also apply conclusions reached in the previous chapter on substance to the current discussion. Recall Aristotle's view that the primary substances are individual living members of species. This point is crucial for understanding Aristotle's philosophy of nature. The natural scientist studies substances that are subject to change. These substances are individual members of species, e.g. this man, that tree, etc. The natural scientist must then explain the principles of natural (as opposed to divine) substances. These natural substances are substances in the primary sense. We must note also that the species and genus terms are substances in a secondary sense. Species and genus terms indicate the real natural kinds into which living things fall. There is thus a direct application of the results of the *Categories* and the *Metaphysics* to the philosophy of nature.

PRINCIPLES OF CHANGE

Things are due to nature, then, if they have an internal source of change or staying unchanged. Aristotle investigates the principles of change by asking what must be the case for change to occur. In raising this question, he tackles an issue that dominated Presocratic and Platonic philosophy. Book 1 of the *Physics* begins with a survey of other views on nature, including those who deny that any change is possible. Though he states that this is not really an issue a natural scientist should discuss, Aristotle nevertheless sets out to refute the view of Parmenides and others that change is impossible. This issue falls outside the bounds of natural science because natural science is premised upon the view that there is a world of change. In beginning our philosophy of nature, we have already assumed the reality of change. For Parmenides, natural science is impossible because it has nothing to study. Change is not real, and there can be no sciences of what is not real. Aristotle challenges this view by providing a definitive refutation of Parmenides' view. What emerge from this refutation are the first principles of the world of change; we thus see another instance of the development of an axiomatic science.

We have one great and difficult poem from Parmenides.[3] Though the poem itself is obscure and at points nearly unintelligible, Parmenides' thought has had an enduring influence on Western philosophy. Plato in particular felt the force of Parmenides' arguments; in order to understand Plato it is essential to understand Parmenides. If we seek to further understand the differences between Plato and Aristotle's views, we must do so in light of Parmenides' extremely influential poem.

Parmenides' poem exhibits a rational model of philosophy; his poem follows a tight and rigorous logic. His poem also ignores all sensory information; one of the main points of his poem is that we cannot trust the information provided by the senses. In following this rational-deductive method, Parmenides purports to prove that generation and destruction are impossible; there is no becoming or ending of the things that are. One of the central insights of Parmenides' great poem is that the notion of non-being is simply incoherent. Generation would seem to suggest that being can arise out of non-being, while destruction suggests that being can degrade into non-being. But if non-being itself is incoherent, then so are these concepts of generation and destruction. Regarding the incoherence of non-being, Aristotle and Parmenides agree; neither holds that we can say anything meaningful or intelligible about non-being. From this point about non-being, however, Parmenides refutes the possibilities of generation and destruction. While Aristotle may agree with Parmenides on the incoherence of non-being, Aristotle rejects the conclusions Parmenides derives. Parmenides' refutation of generation and destruction is extended to a rejection of the possibility of all change. Since the senses reveal a changing world, if change is impossible, then the world revealed by the senses is not real or true. The only reality and truth is revealed by reason; thus begins the rationalist tradition in philosophy. Both Parmenides and Plato maintain that the world revealed by the senses is in some way an illusion; reality is the world as it is revealed to reason, i.e. the intelligible world rather than the sensible world.

Parmenides attempts to demonstrate the impossibility of generation and destruction from a few simple principles. These principles are important because Aristotle also accepts these principles, though Aristotle rejects Parmenides' conclusion. First, Parmenides maintains that nothing can come from nothing; it is not possible for an existing thing to come out of nothing. Second, Parmenides holds that everything is or is not; there is nothing between existence and non-existence. Parmenides also appeals to the principle of sufficient reason, i.e. nothing happens without an explanation or a sufficient reason. This is a core rationalist tenet that we see from ancient through to modern philosophy. Parmenides applies these principles to show that change is impossible. He asks how could something come to be. Either it comes to be out of what is or what is not. It is not possible for something to come from what is not, for nothing can come from nothing. It is not possible for something to come from what is, since what is already is. What is already exists, and so there is no need to generate anything from it. What reason could there be, Parmenides asks, why something which already is would give rise to something else? Since what is already is, it lacks nothing; thus there is no sufficient reason to explain why something would come to be from what is. Therefore, nothing can come to be, since it is not possible to generate something either from what is or what is not; generation and coming to be are impossible. Destruction is proven impossible by similar means. Note the rational elegance of Parmenides' argument. Whatever the senses may tell us, Parmenides holds that reason tells us that change is impossible.

Aristotle seeks to maintain Parmenides' three principles, but he rejects the conclusion reached by Parmenides. In preserving the principles but rejecting the conclusion, Aristotle demonstrates some ingenious argumentative moves that reveal the flaws in Parmenides' purported refutation of change. Consider the problem of generation: how can something come to be? The first possibility is that something comes to be from what is not. Aristotle states:

> Clearly then also to come to be so-and-so from what is not means '*qua* [as] what is not.' It was through failure to make this distinction that those thinkers [Parmenides and his followers] gave the matter up, and through this error that they went so much farther astray as to suppose that nothing else comes to be or exists apart from what is itself, thus doing away with all becoming. We ourselves are in agreement with them in holding that nothing can be said without qualification to come from what is not. But nevertheless we maintain that a thing may come to be from what is not in a qualified sense, i.e. accidentally. For a thing comes to be from the privation, which in its own nature is something which is not – this not surviving as a constituent of the result. (191b8–16)

Aristotle here maintains the principle that nothing can come from nothing. But there is a sense, he argues, in which things come to be out of what is not, namely out of a lack or privation. Things come to be out of what is not, then, not out of nothing, but out of *something which is not*. Aristotle's key insight is to notice that the things that exist have both actuality and potentiality. Existing things actually have some properties, but there are other properties that existing things only potentially have. For example, Socrates actually is snub-nosed and pale; he is potentially a thin-nosed dark person. He does not actually have these latter properties, but he could. Socrates comes to be dark not out of simply nothing; that would run afoul of the requirement that nothing can come from nothing. But he does come to be dark out of a lack or privation, namely the lack of being coloured dark. It is in this respect that Socrates is able to undergo change. He is something; but he is not something that has every property or attribute. It is with respect to the attributes that he lacks that Socrates is able to undergo change. Contrarily, Socrates can lose properties that he has. Every change, then, involves losing some property that one has or gaining some property that one lacks. But these changes are not coming to be out of nothing at all; rather, they are coming to be out of something that has certain properties and lacks others.

Aristotle's main objection to Parmenides, then, concerns the way the latter understands the principle that everything either is or is not. Aristotle argues that Parmenides has understood existence here as predicating all possible properties of a thing. What is cannot come to be anything else because *what is is completely*, i.e. lacking in nothing. Aristotle thus argues that Parmenides slides from treating existence as an all or nothing affair to treating all other forms of predication as all or nothing. To be sure, existence is all or nothing; either something is or is not; there is nothing in between. But it is not the case that because something exists, all possible properties or predications are true of it. Things lack certain properties, and it is with respect to these properties that things are able to undergo change. Aristotle's refutation of Parmenides thus turns on Parmenides' equivocation with respect to *is*; Parmenides treats the *is* of existence in the same way as he treats the *is* of predication. If we keep these distinct, as Aristotle claims we must, then we can see how things can exist and yet undergo changes.

The above discussion may seem difficult at times, but it is really a shining example of Aristotle pointing out a fatal flaw in one of his predecessor's arguments. Treating the *is* of existence and the *is* of predication in the same way led Parmenides to reject the world of change. But this is a logical error, and since Aristotle has made it clear to us, we can now see that the world of change is possible; thus a science of the world of change is possible. There is much at stake for Aristotle in this argument, as there is for Plato and Parmenides. The very possibility of natural science is at stake. Indeed, the very conceptions of philosophy and science are under question: is science a purely rational enterprise, as Plato and Parmenides maintain, or does science draw upon empirical evidence of the senses, as Aristotle maintains? Aristotle has here successfully shown that the rationalist position does not prove what it purports to; the world of the senses is thus saved.

In addition to refuting Parmenides, Aristotle's discussion reveals the first principles of change. These are the first principles of a science of nature. We thus witness the emergence of the axioms of natural science. If natural science is the science of the world of change, then the first principles of natural science must explain how change occurs. In surveying previous thought, Aristotle states, '[a]ll thinkers then agree in making the contraries principles' (188a19). All change is a movement between opposed properties or characteristics. These opposites can be characterized as the presence or lack of a certain property, e.g. the pale and the dark, the wet and the dry, the light and the heavy, etc. All change is a coming to be from one opposite to another. Aristotle continues:

> For first principles must not be derived from one another nor from anything else, while everything has to be derived from them. But these conditions are fulfilled by the primary contraries, which are not derived from anything else because they are primary, nor from each other because they are contraries. (188a27–30)

These primary opposites thus satisfy the conditions for first principles. Being primary, the primary opposites do not come from anything else; there is thus nothing prior to these primary opposites. Because they are opposites, they do not come from each other. We thus have primary opposites as first principles of nature: for every possible characteristic, there is the presence and the lack of that characteristic.

As further evidence that all change involves primary opposites, Aristotle notes that things always come to be out of their opposite and not some other thing. Consider:

> Our first presupposition must be that in nature nothing acts on, or is acted on by, any other thing at random, nor may anything come from anything else, unless we mean that it does so accidentally. For how could white come to be from musical, unless musical happened to be an attribute of the not-white or of the black? No, white comes from not-white – and not from *any* not-white, but from black or some intermediate. (188a31–188b1)

This may seem like an obvious point, but this point reveals a necessary connection between opposites. If there is to be a change with respect to colour, this cannot come to be out of knowing music or being six-feet tall or anything of the sort; a change in colour can only be from the pale to the dark. This necessary connection is established in the following conclusion:

If this is true, everything that comes to be or passes away comes from, or passes into, its contrary or an intermediate state. But the intermediates are derived from the contraries – colours, for instance, from black and white. Everything, therefore, that comes to be by a natural process is either a contrary or a product of contraries. (188b21–25)

All natural change is thus a change from one opposite to another, or to something in between. We can imagine a continuum of being coloured. At one end of the spectrum is the pale and at the other end is the dark. All colours that come to be are in between the pale and the dark. All change with respect to colour involves a change along the continuum between the pale and the dark.

Aristotle refers to this primary opposition as excess and defect, which we have called the presence and the lack. Aristotle states that it is a very difficult question whether to consider the primary opposites as one principle or as two. The opposites are not the same thing, and so it would seem impossible to represent both opposites with one principle. The opposites also, however, have a necessary connection between them; representing the opposites with two separate principles, i.e. one for excess and one for defect, would seem to ignore this necessary connection. The opposites are necessarily paired, and this is not clearly conveyed by treating them as separate principles. Nevertheless, whether we formulate the primary opposites as one principle or as two, it is clear that primary opposites are involved in all change.

Aristotle states, however, that the primary opposites are not enough to explain any change. After all, the pale does not become the dark, nor does the light become the heavy. Rather, the pale is always pale, and the dark is always dark, etc. What happens in all change is instead that *some thing* is acted upon. There must be a natural substance that undergoes the change and persists through the change. There is a thing that is pale that becomes a thing that is dark; the pale does not become dark, but instead some underlying thing moves from one opposite to another or to something in between. In addition to the principle of excess and defect, then, Aristotle postulates *the one* underlying thing that is acted upon (189b13). This rounds out the discussion of the necessary conditions for any change or staying unchanged: there must be a thing acted upon, and it is this thing that changes from one opposite to another or to something in between. The principles of natural science, then, are 'the One and excess and defect' (189b13).

To describe any change, there are three elements. First, there is the one, i.e. the substance that undergoes the change. This substance persists as a reidentifiable subject of change. Socrates pale and Socrates dark is still the same Socrates; we can identify him before the change and identify him as the same subject after the change. The second element in any description of change is the characteristic of the substance before the change; the third element is the characteristic of the substance after the change. The general form of change then is 'S qualified as not-A becomes S qualified as A', where S represents substance and A represents attribute. Consider Aristotle's example of a man who comes to know music. The complete and proper description of this process takes the following form: a man who does not know music comes to be a man who knows music. Though the man who does not know music is numerically one, there are two accounts of him: there is the account of a man, which remains after the change; there is also the account of not knowing music, and this account does not remain after the change. There is thus an underlying substance that persists through the change, as the account of man illustrates. By making explicit the substance undergoing the change and the nature of the change in one of its characteristics, Aristotle avoids the difficulties surrounding change that befell his predecessors.

THE FOUR CAUSES OR EXPLANATIONS (*AITIAI*)

We now understand the first principles of any change or staying unchanged in the natural world. Natural science studies the causes of physical change, and so Aristotle's next topic is to delineate the types of causes involved in all physical change. We only have knowledge when we can answer the question *on account of what?* This gives rise to Aristotle's famous doctrine of the four causes. We face several difficulties in coming to terms with this doctrine of the four causes. This view is presented in *Physics* 3.2 almost without explanation or justification; we must thus supplement Aristotle's discussion to provide the reasons why these four and only these four causes are involved in any natural change. In addition, there is the difficulty in translating the key term in this doctrine: *aitia* (singular) and *aitiai* (plural). *Aitia* does not align exactly with our modern notion of a cause. For Aristotle, *aitia* can mean *cause, reason* or *explanation*. Understanding this point should help us to keep in mind what this doctrine is supposed to explain. Aristotle does not suggest that any natural change has four separate *causes*; rather, he maintains that for any natural changes there are four explanations that must be given. The student of nature must investigate and account for each of these four explanations. Only with these four explanations given can we understand any natural change or staying unchanged.

Consider the following passage in which Aristotle lays out the four types of causes:

> In one way, then, that out of which a thing comes to be and which persists, is called a cause, e.g. the bronze of the statue, the silver of the bowl, and the genera of which the bronze and the silver are species.
>
> In another way, the form of the archetype, i.e. the definition of the essence, and its genera, are called causes (e.g. of the octave the relation of 2:1, and generally number, and the parts in the definition).
>
> Again, the primary source of the change or rest; e.g. the man who deliberated is a cause, the father is the cause of the child, and generally what makes of what is made and what changes of what is changed.
>
> Again, in the sense of end or that for the sake of which a thing is done, e.g. health is the cause of walking about. ('Why is he walking about?' We say: 'To be healthy', and, having said that, we think we have assigned the cause.) (194b23–35)

We shall identify these four causes as the 1) material, 2) formal, 3) efficient and 4) final. The material and formal causes or explanations should by now be familiar. About any natural substance that changes or stays unchanged, we can ask what it is made of and what is its shape, plan or structure. In answering the former question we give a material explanation; in answering the latter we give a formal explanation. Both of these explanations are integral and necessary for understanding any change or staying unchanged.

The efficient cause aligns most closely with our modern conception of a cause; this is the primary source of the change or staying unchanged. There are two basic relationships expressed in the efficient cause. In human action, the efficient cause describes the relationship between the agent and the thing done. The person who deliberates and chooses a course of action is the efficient cause of that action. This can also include the human production of an artefact; the carpenter is the efficient cause of a house. He is the primary source of the change. Second, the efficient cause also expresses the relationship in nature between the producer of change and the thing changed.[4] This relationship is not confined to human action, but rather is a more general relationship in nature. Aristotle's example of the father being the efficient cause of the child applies here. The father is the primary source of the change, i.e. the production of a new substance.[5] While the material and formal causes are internal to the thing undergoing change, the efficient cause is external. The father is external to the child, and the carpenter is external to the house. Compare this to the way in which the matter and form of a child are internal to the child; likewise the bricks and mortar and the form of a house are internal to the house. The matter and form are the inseparable parts of the composite thing that is either a child or a house. While the efficient cause can be external to the thing changed, this is not necessary. Recall that for Aristotle natural substances have within them a source of change or staying unchanged. When we ask what is the efficient cause of the growth and maturation of a human infant, we need not appeal to anything external to the infant. The human infant grows and matures according to its own internal nature.

We now reach the final cause. This cause gains its name from the Latin word *finis*, which means *end* or *aim*; this corresponds to the Greek word *telos*. This cause reveals Aristotle's teleological conception of nature. With respect to any change or staying unchanged, we can ask *on account of what* or *the cause for the sake of which*. In answering these questions, we provide an explanation of the end or goal (*telos*) of the change or staying unchanged. For Aristotle, all natural processes aim at some good for the natural substance involved in the process. Each natural substance pursuing its ends is doing its part in furthering the supreme good of the whole of nature. These ends are due to the natural substance's nature; recall that natural substances have within them a source of change. When we ask why a person walks, we need not appeal to any ends outside of the person. As a human being, the person's health is a benefit to herself or himself. Thus a person walks to achieve the end of health.

Still, there is something a bit peculiar about Aristotle's notion of a final cause. We normally only ascribe goals or ends to conscious rational agents; we say that a person aims at some end only if he or she intends to achieve that end. Thus intentionality seems to be a mark of ends or goals. Aristotle's view on final causes thus seems vulnerable to the objection of anthropocentrism. In treating natural substances as having ends, Aristotle treats them as if they were conscious rational agents with intentions; thus Aristotle treats all natural substances as if they were human agents with goals. But Aristotle rejects the idea that intentions are a mark of goal-directed processes. For Aristotle, every regular natural process, whether intentional or not, aims at some end. We can recall the earlier example regarding a spider constructing a web. Aristotle does not ascribe any conscious intentions to the spider; nevertheless, he still wants to claim that the spider's behaviour is goal-directed. The spider performs this behaviour repeatedly; this behaviour regularly results in the capturing of prey. Is it merely an accident that this process happens over and over again, or does this process actually aim at some goal? The very regularity of this process suggests to Aristotle that the process really aims at a goal; ends and goals are thus a part of the real fabric of nature.

For Aristotle, teleology does not commit the error of anthropocentrism. We do not look at natural substances and processes and treat them as human-like; instead, all of nature is goal-directed, as we can see from the very regularity of these processes. Thus human intentions are a subset of the larger set of all natural processes. The anthropocentric objection would seem to be most damaging if Aristotle were using human intentional processes as the paradigm for all natural processes. According to this objection, Aristotle is taking something distinctive of the human realm and applying it to the rest of nature. I have suggested, however, that these human intentions are one type of goal-directed process. The human is thus not the paradigm for the natural; the natural is goal-directed, and the human is one instantiation of that.

We thus have compiled a list of the four causes or explanations that the student of nature investigates. Together these four causes provide a complete account of any natural process. These four causes can be understood as the necessary conditions for any change or staying unchanged. There is no natural process that can occur without all four of these causes or explanations in place. Separately, then, these four causes are not sufficient to account for any change or staying unchanged.[6]

The relations among the four causes or explanations need to be discussed. Aristotle gives some indications of the relationships among these four causes:

> The last three [formal, efficient and final] often coincide; for the what and that for the sake of which are one, while the primary source of motion is the same in species as these (198a25–26).

This passage seems to suggest the identity of formal and final causes; we can call the cause that results from this identity the formal-final cause. Aristotle identifies these causes because the final cause is in a sense contained in the formal cause. Consider a human infant. The form of a human being is present in the infant. The form of a human being also contains within it the ultimate goal of the human infant, i.e. to mature and achieve human flourishing. This end is common to all things that possess the form of a human being. So in a crucial sense, the ends of a thing are part of the form of a thing. While Aristotle's analysis succeeds with respect to reproduction, it is also successful in explaining familiar natural changes such as movement. Consider a rock. The form of a rock is to have a particular sensible shape as well as a certain structure. Contained within the form of a rock is the fact that, due to its matter, it tends to move downward. Its goal or final cause is thus to move downward towards the centre of the earth. The connection between the formal and final cause thus applies to all natural changes. It is perhaps too strong to suggest that the formal and final causes are identical. The form of a thing explains more than just the ends of a thing. Rather than suggesting strict identity, it seems instead that the final cause is contained in the formal cause. In explaining the plan or structure of a thing, we must include the ends towards which the thing strives.

Aristotle also suggests that the efficient cause is the same in form as the formal and final causes. The example of the human infant is illustrative here as well. The efficient cause of the human infant is the father; it is he who imparts the form to the child. In order to impart the form of a human being, the father must himself embody the form of a human being. The form of the efficient cause, then, is the same as the form of the formal-final cause. A similar relationship obtains with the production of artefacts. In order to produce a statue, the artisan must put the form into the matter; she must shape the bronze. This form that the artisan imparts is already present in the mind of the artisan. Thus the efficient cause, i.e. the artist, contains within her the form that is imparted to the statue. In both nature and art, the efficient cause is the same in form as the formal-final cause.

As a final point, we should note that nowhere does Aristotle suggest that one type of cause excludes another. These four causes or explanations are thus not mutually exclusive, but rather mutually complementary. We cannot ignore material explanations in favour of teleological ones, nor can we ignore material explanations in favour of formal or efficient explanations. Aristotle's emphasis on teleological explanation in nature should thus not be seen as a rejection of any kind of mechanistic explanation. The mechanism proposed by Democritus and the atomists explains something real in nature; it explains the motion, shape and size of the material constituents of natural objects. But according to Aristotle, the mechanism of atomism could not account for the regularity and structure found in nature. The behaviour of whole organisms cannot be captured by appeal to the constitutive elements of the whole. To fully comprehend this regularity and structure, we must offer formal-final explanation as well as material and efficient.

DEFENCE OF TELEOLOGY

Aristotle noted that his predecessors recognized the material, formal and efficient causes, but many rejected the notion of a final cause. Aristotle considered the final cause to be one of his significant contributions to explanation in natural science. Aristotle must, however, justify the inclusion of final causes. He takes up this task in *Physics* 2.8, and it is here that he provides some of his clearest reasoning for why there are ends in nature. He begins by stating, '[w]e must explain then first why nature belongs to the class of causes which act for the sake of something' (198b10). Why not simply conclude that nature has no purposes or ends, i.e. that nature is not for something? Here is Aristotle's presentation of the question:

> A difficulty presents itself: why should not nature work, not for the sake of something, nor because it is better so, but just as the sky rains, not in order to make the corn grow, but of necessity? (What is drawn up must cool, and what has been cooled must become water and descend, the result of this being that the corn grows.) Similarly if a man's crop is spoiled on the threshing-floor, the rain

did not fall for the sake of this – in order that the crop might be spoiled – but the result just followed. Why then should it not be the same with the parts in nature, e.g. that our teeth should come up of necessity – the front teeth sharp, fitted for tearing, the molars broad and useful for grinding down the food – since they did not arise for this end, but it was merely a coincident result; and so with all other parts in which we suppose that there is a purpose? (198b16–29)

In this passage Aristotle gives voice to the objections that may be raised by Democritus, Empedocles and other like-minded philosophers. Why not view nature as mechanical necessity rather than as purposive? For Aristotle, nature is purposive and the ultimate purpose is the good of the natural substances themselves. If we recall our example of why a person walks, Aristotle says that the person walks for health; that is the end and this end is better for the person than the contrary of health. Opposed to this type of explanation is the way we view the rain. We do not claim that the rain falls for a purpose or because it is better; rather the rain falls because it must, i.e. it is necessary. The matter demands that the rain falls. Upon being heated, water evaporates and rises. As it rises, it cools, turns to water and falls. This is not purposive behaviour; rather, it is a clear example of mechanical necessity. It is merely a coincidence that the corn grows after the rain falls; this is not a goal or end of the rain falling.

In contrast to this example of mechanical necessity, Aristotle considers the apparent adaptations of the parts of animals. Aristotle's keen interest in biology was driven at least in part by the fact that biology seems best to exhibit ends in nature; living organisms have parts that seem perfectly adapted to serve the animal's overall well-being. In the above passage, Aristotle notes that animals have sharp front teeth that seem to be for biting and broad back teeth that seem to be for chewing; is it merely an accident or a mechanical necessity that animals have these adaptations, or are these adaptations serving some real end for the animal? It is certainly fascinating to witness Aristotle's attempts to explain one of the most remarkable features of the natural world, i.e. the extraordinary adaptations of living things. It would be two millennia before Darwin's theory of evolution through natural selection adequately explained the adaptations of living things, but there is still much to learn from Aristotle's attempts to come to terms with the observational evidence.

Let us consider Aristotle's argument for the existence of final causes in nature. The following argument is presented in *Physics* 2.8:

> For teeth and all other natural things either invariably or for the most part come about in a given way; but of not one of the results of chance or spontaneity is this true. We do not ascribe to chance or mere coincidence the frequency of rain in winter, but frequent rain in summer we do; nor heat in summer but only if we have it in winter. If then, it is agreed that things are either the result of coincidence or for the sake of something, and these cannot be the result of coincidence or spontaneity, it follows that they must be for the sake of something; and that such things are all due to nature even the champions of the theory which is before us would agree. Therefore action for an end is present in things which come to be and are by nature. (198b35–199a8)

The above argument for ends in nature hinges upon the thesis of regularity. Things due to nature happen with regularity, i.e. always or for the most part. It is a regular occurrence, for example, that humans are born with two hands, or that animals have sharp teeth in front and broad teeth in back. Things due to chance or luck do not happen with regularity. We thus see chance occurrences against the backdrop of regularity and order in nature. When we say that something is due to chance, we are stating that some occurrence does not fit with the regularity and order of nature.

Aristotle also presents the dichotomy that things are either for something or due to chance. Either things happen regularly or they do not; if the former, they are due to nature; if the latter, they are due to chance. This dichotomy is key in Aristotle's argument, though we might wonder whether he has set up a false dichotomy. Perhaps there are forms of regularity that are not *for something*. For example, the case of the rain falling is an instance of something that happens regularly, but it does not happen *for something*. Cases of mechanical necessity, i.e. a process necessitated by the matter involved, seem to be clear examples of regularity that are not for something. This suggests that the third premise should be something of the following form: things either happen regularly or by chance; if regular, they may be due to mechanical necessity or for something. Thus Aristotle's argument has not proven what it purports to; there are possible forms of regularity that are not for something. Aristotle needs to prove that there are forms of regularity that are for something. He also needs to make room for forms of regularity that are due to necessity. This argument does not establish these conclusions, but Aristotle never wavers in his conviction that nature exhibits regularities that are for something and regularities that are necessary.

While the argument given in *Physics* 2.8 is not completely successful, it does provide a clear indication of the reasoning that leads Aristotle to his conclusion. The permanence of species is for Aristotle a clear example of regularity in nature. Species breed true to type; monstrous births, as Aristotle refers to them, are irregular and exceptional. These exceptions prove the rule that things due to nature happen always or for the most part. In addition to animals and plants breeding true to type, it is also the case that each successive generation of living things uses their parts to serve the same ends as their ancestors. Thus successive generations of human beings all employ their hands for the same ends; likewise successive generations of spiders all employ their webs towards the same ends. If a process constantly produces end-like results without final causes being present, we would rightly view this as incredible. Thus if a process is constantly producing end-like results, it is because the process actually aims at some end. There can still be mistakes; nature is not perfect, which is why ends are achieved always or for the most part. But if there is no impediment, then the ends are achieved.

There also does not need to be any evidence of deliberation in achieving ends. Consider the following passage:

> This [the existence of ends in nature] is most obvious in the animals other than man: they make things neither by art nor after inquiry or deliberation. That is why people wonder whether it is by intelligence or some other faculty that these creatures work – spiders, ants, and the like. By gradual advance in this direction we come to see clearly that in plants too that is produced which conduces to the end – leaves e.g., grow to provide shade for the fruit. If then it is both by nature and for an end that the swallow makes its nest and the spider its web, and plants grow leaves for the sake of the fruit and send their roots down (not up) for the sake of nourishment, it is plain that this kind of cause is operative in things which come to be and are by nature. And since nature is twofold, the matter and the form, of which the latter is the end, and since all the rest is for the sake of the end, the form

must be the cause in the sense of that for the sake of which. (199a20–32)

This passage confirms that Aristotle's teleology concerns purposes without minds. At first glance this seems like a contradictory thesis; what does it mean, after all, to suggest that there are purposes in nature that are not the purposes of any mind? If we cannot say that the living organism in some sense *sees itself* as achieving or striving for some end or purpose, then how can we state that such ends really exist? Aristotle resists the idea that the purposes are contained in god's mind or any other intelligence. God does not intervene to see that animals and plants strive for their ends and survival. The form of a living organism is all that is needed to explain its striving for survival; we need appeal to no external intelligence or force. Aristotle thus seems forced into the teleological view that there are purposes in nature that are not the purposes of any mind. Living things strive for their own benefit and survival, and they regularly employ certain parts in achieving this end. Though intentions are usually considered to be a mark of purposive behaviour, Aristotle argues instead that any regular behaviour, whether intentional or not, actually does aim at some end. Regularity, not intentionality, is the mark of ends in nature.

The above passage also highlights Aristotle's contention that 'all the rest is for the sake of the end' (199a32). On this view, every part of a living thing is for the end, i.e. the survival and benefit of each particular living thing. The parts thus must be seen in light of the whole. The formal cause describes the whole. The form describes the shape, plan or structure of a given thing. The form contains within it the end of the whole; this conclusion was reached when Aristotle linked the formal cause with the final cause. Aristotle's basic view, then, is that the student of nature must understand the whole organism and how the parts of the organism contribute to the end of the organism. Everything about the organism is directed towards this end.

Aristotle also appeals to another line of reasoning to establish the reality of ends in nature. He argues that natural substances strive insofar as is possible to participate in the divine. At first this claim is puzzling; how are mortal creatures to participate in the divine? We must recall that for Aristotle species are permanent types. Thus the species is in a sense immortal.[7] Each organism, then, is a part of an immortal species. In living, maturing and reproducing, each organism is participating in the divine insofar as it is possible (415a29). The ends of each organism, then, are ultimately a striving towards immortality. In acting to benefit itself, each organism contributes to the supreme good in nature.

These issues surrounding Aristotle's teleology are among the most difficult and controversial in his work. These issues also remain central to contemporary debates in the philosophy of biology. Though evolutionary theory rejects the notion of design, some philosophers and biologists maintain that there are real purposes, functions or ends in nature; in other words, it is still a matter of debate whether the adaptations of animals are for something. Contemporary biology faces a problem similar to Aristotle's; in rejecting design, contemporary biology also considers whether there can be purposes or ends without design. We have seen how Aristotle attempted to establish the reality of purposes without minds on the basis of the regularity of biological adaptations. Even though there has been a radical shift in our biological thinking from the Aristotelian to the Darwinian, the problem of explaining the adaptations of organisms has not yet been resolved. There is still a basic disagreement over an issue that also vexed Aristotle: whether the adaptations of living organisms are for something or are due to chance.

We have thus surveyed several of the key philosophical issues in Aristotle's philosophy of nature. Now that we understand the definition of nature, the principles of change in nature, and the causes or explanations in nature, we are prepared for study in Aristotle's works in natural science. The foundation provided in this chapter thus equips us for a study of Aristotle's biological works: *Parts of Animals*, *Movement of Animals* and *Generation of Animals*. In these works, we see evidence of Aristotle fulfilling the scientific project laid out in *Physics*. The remaining works dealt with in the next two chapters, i.e. *De Anima* and *Nicomachean Ethics*, also draw heavily upon the findings of *Physics*. In *De Anima*, Aristotle provides his account of soul, which is the mark of living natural substances. In *Nicomachean Ethics*, Aristotle concentrates on the end or goal of human life; he argues that human life aims at *eudaimonia*, which means *flourishing* or *well-being*. It is taken as a given, already established in *Physics*, that all living things strive towards some end; humans are no exception to this law of nature. Thus the mode of analysis of natural substances developed in *Physics* is directly applicable to the study of soul and the study of human flourishing.

This is one of the great benefits of a systematic approach to Aristotle's thought. We began with the general science of substance that applies to divine substances and natural substances. The truths uncovered in first philosophy are true for all other fields of science. Thus first philosophy reveals the law of non-contradiction. We know, then, that for any substance, whether natural or divine, it is not possible for a contradiction to be true of that substance. After first philosophy, we study second philosophy; all the truths of second philosophy apply to all the subordinate natural sciences. Thus second philosophy reveals the principles involved in all change: the one, excess and deficiency. Any change – whether in biology, botany, chemistry or any other natural science – must accord with the account of change given in *Physics*. Further, any change or staying unchanged must be accounted for by appeal to the four causes or explanations. The progress made in second philosophy thus enables a systematic approach to soul and human flourishing as well as all other subjects that fall under the heading of natural science. Given that we still have a keen interest in explaining the natural world, Aristotle's foundational ideas about matter, form, ends and change remain central to our attempts to understand the natural world. It is in *Physics* that Aristotle lays out this robust and compelling scientific programme for investigating nature. Many of the ideas central to this programme remain with us today, either as vital parts of our explanatory apparatus or as hotly contested concepts. Aristotle is not the dominant figure he once was in natural science, but his influence remains.

CHAPTER 4

SOUL (*PSUCHE*)

With a general understanding of the science of nature established, we now move on to the study of one of the most extraordinary and wondrous features of the natural world: life. In the realm of nature, there is a key distinction between that which lives and that which does not. What differentiates the living from the non-living is the presence of soul (*psuche*). Our investigation into soul is thus firmly rooted in natural science; the study of soul is part of the philosophy of nature we began in the previous chapter. We are asking what explains the life of natural substances. Consider Aristotle's opening lines of *On the Soul*:

> Holding as we do that, while knowledge of any kind is a thing to be honoured and prized, one kind of it may, either by reason of its greater exactness or of a higher degree of dignity and greater wonderfulness in its objects, be more honourable and precious than any other, on both accounts we should naturally be led to place in the front rank the study of the soul. The knowledge of the soul admittedly contributes greatly to the advance of truth in general, and above all, to our understanding of Nature, for the soul is in some sense the principle of animal life. (402a1–7)[1]

Knowledge of soul is thus of the first rank because of the exactness we may achieve and because of the superior and more remarkable subject of our study. I remarked earlier that Aristotle's introductions to various subjects often reveal a sense of wonder and amazement; this is evident in his introduction to soul. Aristotle introduces us to the study not of some arcane or dry subject matter; rather, we are here studying perhaps the most fascinating and marvellous subject of all. Though life may be pervasive in nature, it still inspires awe in Aristotle.

The earliest Greek philosophers accepted the basic view that anything that lives has soul; Aristotle also accepts this view. Plants, trees, insects, animals and human beings thus all have souls. This understanding of soul conflicts with many modern approaches to soul. Thus the first difficulty we experience in approaching this aspect of Aristotle's thought concerns the modern connotations of the word *soul*. For example, two thousand years of Christian theology have helped to establish the notion that only human beings have souls. This religious sense of soul usually implies that the soul is essentially moral and rational. The religious conception of soul thus ascribes souls to only those animals that are created in the image and likeness of god; these animals are human beings with the properties of rationality, intentionality, consciousness and moral judgement. Some religious and philosophical views also maintain the immortality of the soul. While Aristotle would agree that human souls have the property of rationality, he would reject the notion that all souls must possess rationality. In general, the religious sense of soul under discussion here emphasizes a difference between the human and the rest of nature. Aristotle's view, which he shares with a long tradition of Greek philosophers, emphasizes instead the similarities that all living things share.

The word *soul* thus brings with it several connotations that are unhelpful for approaching Aristotle's *On the Soul*. Rather than using the word *soul*, some scholars of Aristotle suggest that we instead use the word *animator*. This derives from the Latin verb *animare*, which means, *to instil with life*. This verb is also the source of the Latin title of Aristotle's work, *De Anima*. Rather than translating this title into English as *On the Soul*, we might opt instead for *On the Animator*. This is somewhat clumsier and less familiar, though it does avoid some of the connotations that come with *soul*. We might also opt to use the Greek term *psuche* as a way of avoiding the difficulties with *soul*. In this chapter, I shall use the standard and received word *soul*. As long as we are aware that Aristotle's conception of soul does not mean the same thing as some religious or philosophical conceptions of soul, we shall avoid any serious confusion. For Aristotle, the soul is the first principle of life, but life requires much more than the rational or moral properties attributed to the soul by certain theological and philosophical views.

Aristotle holds that the soul is a cluster of capacities specific to each species. For Aristotle, the varieties of souls can be ordered hierarchically based on the capacities possessed by each species. The most basic capacity that all living things possess is the capacity for self-nourishment (415a23). In order to live, an organism must be able to take in nourishment from outside itself. Without this capacity, nothing lives. This capacity for nourishment explains the growth and decay of a living thing. A second capacity basic to all living things is the capacity for reproduction. All organisms produce offspring like them. In some sense, nourishment and reproduction are the same capacity; an organism nourishes itself not only so that it may grow and survive, but also so that it may reproduce. As we saw in the discussion of *Physics*, it is through reproduction that living things participate in the divine insofar as they can; each organism contributes to the eternal and immutable species. Plant life exhibits only this capacity for nourishment and reproduction; the plant soul is thus the simplest soul. While plants exhibit only this capacity, there are higher animals that exhibit additional capacities. Animals, for example, also exhibit the capacities for movement and perception. In perceiving, animals also have desire; animals can perceive pleasure and pain, and they naturally desire to feel pleasure and avoid pain. Finally, there is the highest capacity of soul, which is the capacity for thought. Only human beings possess this capacity. But of course, this is not the only capacity we possess; we must also have the capacities for nourishment, reproduction, movement and perception.

Some philosophical commentators who treat Aristotle's *On the Soul* consider his views under the headings of *psychology* or *philosophy of mind*. These labels contribute to a general misunderstanding of Aristotle's project in *On the Soul*. Psychology and philosophy of mind emphasize the uniquely human. While it is true that the word *psychology* derives from the Greek term *psuche*, modern psychology tends to focus on the human properties of perception, rationality and emotion. Psychology is thus principally the study of the human psyche; Aristotle's *On the Soul* includes the study of the human psyche, but his project encompasses all other kinds of souls as well. Modern psychology is mainly concerned with mental properties; Aristotle's treatment of soul considers all capacities of soul. Living things must have properties other than mental ones; indeed, only a few living things can properly be said to have mental properties. Living things must also nourish themselves, grow and reproduce;

these functions of living things are not the focus of modern psychology, but they are fundamental to Aristotle's account of soul. Considering *On the Soul* under this heading thus obscures the hierarchical conception of soul presented by Aristotle; certainly the higher capacity of thought is a part of the study of soul, but it is not the entirety of the subject.

Considering Aristotle's views in *On the Soul* under the heading of philosophy of mind is also misleading. To be sure, Aristotle does treat issues relating to philosophy of mind; he considers the nature of thought, for example. But we shall find little overlap between Aristotle's *On the Soul* and modern problems in philosophy of mind. Aristotle is not concerned, for example, to explain consciousness or intentionality. Aristotle's treatment of soul is also not primarily epistemological. He does not investigate soul in an attempt to justify human knowledge; Aristotle does not try to show how perceptions can be relied upon, for example, or how we can trust certain judgements. These are among the most contentious topics in contemporary philosophy of mind, but these issues are not treated in *On the Soul*. We should not, however, expect Aristotle to conform to our concerns in philosophy of mind. After all, it is not Aristotle's intention to give a philosophy of mind in *On the Soul*; rather, his goal is to provide an account of soul. While some modern religious and philosophical thinkers identify the mind with the soul, such an identity is far from Aristotle's own view. It is thus more appropriate to undertake our investigation under the following headings: philosophy of soul or philosophy of life. These headings indicate more clearly and faithfully Aristotle's project in *On the Soul*.

SOUL AS SUBSTANCE, FORM AND ACTUALITY

Book 1 of *On the Soul* follows a familiar Aristotelian pattern: he surveys the views of earlier thinkers and the puzzles into which their theories fell. In Book 2.1 of *On the Soul*, Aristotle begins his own account of soul:

> Let the foregoing suffice as our account of the views concerning the soul which have been handed down by our predecessors; let us now make as it were a completely fresh start, endeavouring to answer the question, What is soul? i.e. to formulate the most general possible account of it. (412a1–5)

Chapters 1–3 of Book 2 provide Aristotle's answers to these questions. His conclusion is that soul is substance, form and actuality. In this section, we shall explore how each of these terms applies to soul. Chapters 1 and 2 of Book 2 both serve as introductions to Aristotle's account of soul; each chapter treats similar issues, though the manner of expression is slightly different. The likely reason for this overlap is that these chapters were two different introductions to Aristotle's account of soul from different lectures he gave. Fortunately, while the order of topics and manner of expression differs, the general conclusions reached by these first two chapters point to a coherent account of soul.

Aristotle begins by raising some familiar distinctions to locate the soul. Invoking the discussions from the *Metaphysics*, Aristotle says that things are spoken of as substance in three ways: substance as matter, substance as form and substance as the compound of matter and form. If soul is thought to be substance, Aristotle reasons, it must be substance in one of these three senses. Aristotle reminds us 'matter is potentiality, form [is] actuality' (412a9). Matter could be anything; it is thus purely potential. It is only when form is present that something that is *potentially* so-and-so becomes *actually* so-and-so. The matter of flesh and bone is only potentially a living body; when form is present, it is then an actually living body. But we say that something has a soul not when it is potentially alive, but when it actually lives. This suggests to Aristotle that the soul cannot be the matter of a thing:

> Hence the rightness of the view that the soul cannot be without a body, while it cannot *be* a body; it is not a body but something relative to a body. That is why it is *in* a body, and a body of a definite kind. (414a20–21)

The soul, then, is not body but is related to body; the soul of an organism is not the matter, but it is related to the matter and exists in the matter. What is clear from Aristotle's attempt to locate the soul is that the soul is actuality, whereas body and matter are only potentiality. His next task is to determine what kind of actuality the soul is.

Aristotle dismisses matter as the soul of a living thing; he also rejects the idea that the compound of matter and form is the soul of a living thing. The compound of matter and form is posterior; the compound is the living thing that arises from the compound of matter and form. The matter and the form are thus logically and explanatorily prior to the compound of matter and form. But Aristotle has already claimed that the soul is considered the first principle of life. It is not possible, then, that the first principle of life could be something posterior. The first principle of life must be something prior to the compound of matter and form; soul must be either matter or form. We have already seen Aristotle's arguments rejecting matter as soul. With matter and the compound of matter and form eliminated, Aristotle settles on soul as form.

This line of reasoning leads Aristotle to his first major conclusion about soul: 'Hence the soul must be a substance in the sense of the form of a natural body having life potentially within it. But substance is actuality, and thus soul is the actuality of a body as above characterized' (412a20–22). Soul is substance in the sense of form; soul is not matter or the compound of matter and form. Soul is the principle of structure of a living thing, i.e. its plan or design. Further, soul is the form of a particular kind of body, namely that which potentially could be alive. But we say that soul is present not when a body is potentially alive, but when it actually is alive. Soul is then a kind of actuality; soul is the realization of the potential for life. We can consider this point in light of the fantastic example of Dr Frankenstein and his monster. Before it is alive, the monster has the potential for life; it has all the appropriate organs and matter and they are arranged in the appropriate ways. When life is imparted to the monster, what was once potentially a living thing is now an actually living thing. The monster has the capacities to nourish itself, move, perceive and think; at this point soul is present. Of course this example is fiction, but it illustrates well the difference between matter, which is only potential, and form, which is actual.

Aristotle's view on living things is often referred to as *hylemorphism*, which derives from the Greek words *hyle* (matter) and *morphe* (form). It is not the case that living things are composed of two separate things, i.e. a body and a soul. Rather, a living thing is a complex unity that we can analyse in terms of its matter and its form. As we have seen before in Aristotle's first philosophy and second philosophy, matter and form are not separable in reality. They are only separable in thought. That is to say, we can think about living things in terms of their matter and their form, but there are never living things that possess only matter or only form. What it means to be a living thing is to be a complex unity of ensouled matter or embodied soul. Aristotle's view is thus importantly distinct from dualist views about living things that conceive of the body and soul as separate entities. There are a variety of dualist views about the body and soul; these views conceive of the living thing as being composed of two distinct entities or substances, i.e. body and soul. Platonic and Cartesian dualisms, as well as the traditional Christian conception of the soul, are examples of this approach. On these views, the soul is its own substance that can exist separately from the body; in a sense, the soul is substance that is imprisoned in another substance, i.e. the body. This is not Aristotle's view. For Aristotle, the soul is substance in the sense that the soul has being or reality; the soul is not substance in the sense that it is separable and self-subsistent. Aristotle states that soul is 'substance in the sense of the form of a natural body'; thus soul is not substance as a separable and individual entity, but rather soul is substance as the form of a natural body (412a20). Both the form and the natural body are required for the complex unity that is a living natural substance. For Aristotle, the soul is not a substance imprisoned in the body; rather, the soul is the particular plan, shape and capacities of a body.

Aristotle further clarifies the sense in which soul is actuality. He distinguishes between two kinds of actuality. First actuality (*hexis*) is the presence of a capacity that is not being exercised. Aristotle likens first actuality to knowledge; we can be said to have knowledge even when we are not actively thinking about that knowledge. Knowledge, then, can be present in us as something we could be exercising but are not. Second actuality (*energia*) is the exercising of a capacity. When a thing is using one of its capacities, that capacity exhibits second actuality. Aristotle likens second actuality to contemplation. It is the nature of contemplation to be exercised; we do not say that a person contemplates unless they are actually exercising their capacity for contemplation. Thus it is the nature of contemplation to be exercised, while it is the nature of knowledge to be possessed without necessarily being exercised. Aristotle asks to which type of actuality does soul belong. Based on this distinction, it is clear that soul is first actuality; soul is present when a thing has certain capacities but is not necessarily exercising them. It is not the nature of soul to be exercising certain capacities; soul can be present even when the capacities of soul are not being exercised. We can be asleep and not exercising our capacities, though the capacities are present. To be sure, Aristotle's point here seems to be in error; it is not the case that a soul can be exercising none of its capacities. Even when we are asleep, there are some capacities of soul that are being exercised, such as respiration and growth. For life to be present, it cannot be the case that all capacities of soul are in first actuality. Nevertheless, this leads Aristotle to his most specific definition of soul: 'That is why the soul is an actuality of the first kind of a natural body having life potentially in it', and the soul is 'an actuality of the first kind of a natural organized body' (412a27, 412b5). Though these definitions are worded slightly differently, the basic definition of soul is the same. Soul is the form of a natural body, and it is form in the sense of first actuality.

Aristotle illustrates this definition of soul through two examples. He considers an artefact as if it were a natural substance and he considers a part of an animal as if it were a natural substance. Consider the following:

> Suppose that a tool, e.g. an axe, were a *natural* body, then being an axe would have been its essence, and so its soul; if this disappeared from it, it would have ceased to be an axe, except in name. (412b12–14)

If we consider an axe as a natural body, then the soul of the axe is what it is to be an axe. What makes an axe an axe? What is it to be an axe? The essence or form of an axe is the capacity to cut. If an axe loses this capacity to cut, it is an axe in name only, or as Aristotle says, homonymously. Consider a toy axe. A toy axe is an axe in name only; it is not a real axe because it does not possess what it is to be an axe, i.e. the capacity to cut. Consider Aristotle's next example:

> Next, apply this doctrine in the case of the parts of the living body. Suppose that the eye were an animal – sight would have been its soul, for sight is the substance of the eye which corresponds to the account, the eye being merely the matter of seeing; when seeing is removed the eye is no longer an eye, except in name – no more than the eye of a statue or of a painted figure. (412b17–21)

I propose Figure 2 to show how the examples of the axe and the eye illuminate Aristotle's account of soul:

Compound of Matter and Form	Axe	Eye	Animal
Matter	Wood/Metal	Pupil	Body with Organs
Form/Soul	Capacity to Cut	Capacity to See	First Actuality: Inactivity of Capacities to Nourish, Reproduce, Perceive and Move
	Cutting	Seeing	Second Actuality: Activity of Capacities to Nourish, Reproduce, Perceive and Move

Figure 2. A schematic of the analogies presented at 412b12–21.

From the above schematic, we can see how the soul is the capacity of a certain thing to be what it is. The soul is thus not a thing; it is not a separable and self-subsistent substance. The soul is instead a collection of capacities or powers of a certain kind of body. An axe is an instrument for cutting, an eye is an organ for seeing, and an animal is a natural substance for nourishing, reproducing, moving and perceiving. Note how the form or soul of a natural substance then defines what a thing is in virtue of what it does. What is an animal? It is the kind of thing that has the capacities to nourish itself, reproduce, move and perceive. That is the essence of what it is to be an animal. If something does not have these capacities, it is not an animal, just as an axe that cannot cut is not an axe and an eye that cannot see is not an eye.

We can note that Aristotle's account of soul conceives of soul as the embodied form of a living thing. Indeed, it does not make sense on Aristotle's account to ask whether the soul can exist apart from the body. The soul is not the kind of thing that could be separated from the body; the soul is simply the form in the sense of first actuality of a body with organs. The soul must then be related to body. We can logically distinguish the form from the matter of a living thing, but in reality the form and matter are inseparable. Thus soul and body are inseparable; each living natural substance is a compound of soul and body, form and matter. We have referred to this view as *hylemorphism*. Though this is Aristotle's general view about the soul, he does leave room for an exception to this view. Consider the following remarks:

From this it is clear that the soul is inseparable from its body, or at any rate that certain parts of it are (if it has parts) – for the actuality of some of them is the actuality of the parts themselves. Yet some may be separable because they are not the actualities of any body at all. (413a3–6)

In cases where the actuality is of the parts themselves, i.e. the organs, it is not possible for the soul to be separated from the body. But if there are capacities of the soul that are not actualities of some organ, then it seems possible that those capacities of soul could be separable from the body. When we consider capacities such as sight and hearing, it is clear that there can be no actuality of sight or hearing without the presence of an eye or an ear. The actuality of these capacities is the actuality of certain organs. We reach the same conclusions if we consider the capacities of nourishment, reproduction and movement. There is, however, one capacity of soul that Aristotle regards as separable from the body: thought. We shall treat Aristotle's view on the nature of thought and its separability from the body in the final section of this chapter. For now, let it suffice to say that Aristotle conceives of soul as embodied form inseparable from body, except in the case of thought, which deserves special consideration.

WHAT THE STUDENT OF SOUL INVESTIGATES

Just as Aristotle's *Physics* lays out a research programme for what the student of nature must investigate, so too *On the Soul* lays out the issues that the student of soul must investigate and explain. In *On the Soul*, Aristotle first approaches the research project of the student of soul on analogy with the discipline of geometry. Consider Aristotle's presentation of the analogy between geometry and the study of soul:

It is now evident that a single definition can be given of soul only in the same sense as one can be given of figure. For, as in that case there is no figure apart from triangle and those that follow in order, so here there is no soul apart from the forms of soul just enumerated. It is true that a common definition can be given for figure which will fit all figures without expressing the particular nature of any figure. So here in the case of soul and its specific forms. Hence it is absurd in this and similar cases to look for a common definition which will not express the peculiar nature of anything that is and will not apply to the appropriate indivisible species, while at the same time omitting to look for an account which will. (414b20–28)

In this passage Aristotle makes a number of significant points regarding how the student of soul should proceed. This is a difficult and compressed passage, and in the following I hope to make clear the reasoning that leads Aristotle to his conclusions about the study of soul.

First there is the point that there is only one definition of figure, just as there is only one definition of soul. Geometry studies figure, but geometry studies only specific figures. Geometry does not study some figure over and above all the specific figures; rather, geometers study triangles, quadrilaterals, pentagons, etc. There is a single definition of all of these figures, i.e. a certain number of lines that enclose a space. We can note that this definition of figure is not peculiar to any one figure; rather, it is common to all of them. For this reason, Aristotle says, it is foolish to seek a common definition of figure; we would be seeking a definition that is not peculiar to any one kind of figure. If, for example, we say that we are studying a certain number of lines that enclose a space, it is not at all clear to which kind of figure we are referring. Thus, Aristotle says, geometers do not study a common definition of figure; rather, they study triangle, quadrilateral, pentagon, etc. In Aristotle's terms, they study the proper indivisible species of figures, and they construct accounts of figure based on these indivisible species. Thus geometers seek the account of three-sided figure, of four-sided figure, of five-sided figure, and so on. Note also that on Aristotle's view a useful account of figure is one that is peculiar to some actually existing figure. It is unhelpful to have a definition of figure that does not correspond to some actually existing figure.

Let us apply the above reasoning to the case of soul. Just as there is no figure over and above the specific figures, so also there is no soul over and above the specific souls. We have already arrived at a common definition of soul: soul is the first actuality of a body with organs. We can note that this definition of soul is not peculiar to any specific kind of soul. This definition applies to the souls of plants, animals or humans. Following the analogy with figure, the student of soul thus would not study the common definition of soul. Rather, the student of soul will study the accounts of soul that correspond to the indivisible species. This means that the student of soul must first study the souls of plants; this is the most basic species of soul. Next the student of soul must study the souls of animals that possess perception but lack movement; this is another indivisible species of soul. After this species comes the species of soul pertaining to animals that have perception and movement. Finally, there is the account of soul that corresponds to the human species; this account of soul will include the capacity of thought. So the first conclusion Aristotle establishes regarding the study of the soul is that we should seek accounts of the soul that correspond to the indivisible species of souls. We should always favour a definition that is peculiar to some actually existing thing over a definition that is not peculiar to an actually existing thing. This is the first guideline for the student of soul. We can note how Aristotle's conclusion aligns with his general view about definitions and universal terms. For Aristotle, universal terms exist only insofar as there is some individual thing that instantiates the universal. If there is no such existing thing, then the universal is not real. In the cases of figure and soul, this means that the common definitions of soul and figure are not as real as the definitions of actually existing figures and souls. We thus see how for Aristotle individual existing things have ontological priority; definitions and universals are real only if they provide an account of some actually existing thing.

Continuing with the geometrical analogy, Aristotle notes that there is a logical progression in the way geometers study figure. Geometers study a triangle; they add one line to a triangle to study a quadrilateral; another line is added to study a pentagon; and so on. While the logic of this progression in geometry is clear, Aristotle states that we must explain the succession with respect to souls as well. What logic or reason explains why the plant soul is the most basic, followed by the various types of animal souls? Aristotle states:

> Why the terms are related in this serial way must form the subject of examination. For the power of perception is never found apart from the power of self-nutrition, while – in plants – the latter is found isolated from the former. Again, no sense is found apart from that of touch, while touch *is* found by itself; many animals have neither sight, hearing, nor smell. Again, among living things

that possess sense some have the power of locomotion, some not. Lastly, certain living beings – a small minority – possess calculation and thought, for (among mortal beings) those which possess calculation have all the other powers above mentioned, while the converse does not hold. (415a1–10)

Aristotle's conception of the soul is clearly hierarchical; there are basic capacities that all souls must have, and there are higher and rarer faculties. What explains this hierarchy of capacities in living things? This is a question for the student of soul to answer. The geometer has explained the logical progression of figure; the student of soul must provide a similar explanation for the hierarchy of souls.

In *On the Soul* 2.3, Aristotle lays out a concrete research programme for the study of the soul. We must abandon the quest for a common definition of soul for the reasons mentioned above. What remains is the search for accounts of souls that are peculiar to the indivisible species. The student of soul must thus investigate each indivisible species of soul and determine what are the capacities unique to each species. Recall that for Aristotle the specific cluster of capacities that characterize that species of soul defines each species of soul. In addition to this project, the student of soul must also investigate the hierarchy of souls. Finally, the student of soul must investigate the capacities of souls. Much of the remainder of *On the Soul* is concerned with this latter project. In the following sections of this chapter, we shall examine Aristotle's treatments of the capacities of perception and thought.

PERCEPTION

On the Soul 2.5–12 is concerned with the faculties of sense perception. In these chapters, Aristotle seeks to explain the various kinds of sense perception and how they relate to their objects of perception. Aristotle was not the first to consider the faculties of sense perception; in his discussion, he draws upon several Presocratic theories of sense perception. In general, Aristotle follows the Presocratic tradition in that he provides a physiological and causal theory of perception. As we noted above, Aristotle is not concerned in *On the Soul* to establish the reliability or veracity of perception; his concern is thus not epistemological. Aristotle states that perceptions are always true; if you perceive a tree, you are actually having that perception of a tree (428a10). Aristotle does not concern himself with the question of whether our perceptions actually correspond to the way objects are. His focus is rather on explaining the physiological process of perception; he approaches this process in causal terms, i.e. there is an object of perception that affects our sense organs in some way. In other words, Aristotle is less concerned with how we can know that our perceptions are true than with understanding how perceptions can occur at all. He thus sets out to answer this primary question about perception: what is happening when we perceive something? He reserves for another place discussion of the epistemological question: how can we know that our perceptions are true?

Aristotle accepts the view that sense perception involves being affected in some way. For sense perception to occur, there must be some object external to the senses that affects the sense organ. This explains why the senses do not perceive themselves: the eye does not perceive itself, nor does the ear perceive itself. The senses do not perceive themselves, but rather they perceive some object external to the senses (417a2–5). According to Aristotle, the fact that the senses can only perceive when there is some external object present shows that the senses exist by way of potentiality rather than by way of actuality (417a5). The senses do not actually perceive all of the time; they are potentially such as to perceive, but they only actually perceive when an external object is present. This treatment of perception parallels Aristotle's discussion of first actuality and second actuality with respect to the soul. Perception, as with all capacities of soul, exists as first actuality of a body with organs. Perception thus requires the first actuality of the organs of perception as well as an external object that affects the organs in some way. When an object is present to the organ, the sense organ achieves second actuality.

Aristotle seeks to give a more precise account of being affected or being acted upon. Consider:

> Also the expression 'to be acted upon' has more than one meaning; it may mean either the extinction of one of two contraries by the other, or the maintenance of what is potential by the agency of what is actual and already like what is acted upon, as actual to potential. (417b2–5)

The above quotation is rather compressed and difficult, but it provides an indication of Aristotle's thoughts on the way in which perception involves being affected. Being affected is both a kind of destruction and a kind of preservation. Being affected is a kind of destruction because what is present in the organ of perception before the act of perceiving is destroyed; the organ of perception is affected in that it becomes something else, namely the object of perception. The organ of perception is not the object of perception before the perception occurs; this is why Aristotle says that the destruction is by the contrary. The organ of perception is in a sense destroyed by something contrary to it, i.e. the object of perception. There is also a kind of preservation at work in perception. The organ of perception preserves the object of perception by becoming that object. Before the perception, the organ of perception was only potentially the object of perception; through perception, the organ of perception preserves the object of perception. Being affected is thus both a kind of destruction and a kind of preservation.

Consider an example to help illustrate Aristotle's view on being affected. Imagine the case of a perceiver whose eyes are closed; upon opening her eyes, she perceives a tree. When her eyes are closed, the organ of sight perceives only darkness. The organ of sight has in a way become the darkness. When she opens her eyes and perceives the tree, the darkness that was present in the organ of sight is now destroyed. The darkness has been replaced by the perception of the tree. The perception of the tree is a kind of preservation of the tree; the organ of sight, which was only potentially a tree, now has in a way become the tree. In becoming the tree, the organ of sight preserves the tree; the eye preserves the tree as a perception. This preservation, however, lasts only as long as the perception. Being affected thus involves the destruction of whatever was present in the organ of perception before the perception occurs; it also involves the preservation of the object of perception in the organ of perception for as long as the perception lasts.

The dominant Presocratic view regarding perception is summed up by the phrase *like affects like*. The organs of perception are themselves made up of matter; the pupil, for example, is made of the element water. The view that *like affects like* holds that the organs of perception are only affected by objects of perception that are like the organs, i.e. that are composed of the same elemental material as the organs. We can better understand Aristotle's own view in light of this Presocratic thesis. Aristotle states, 'it is that in one sense, as has already been stated, what acts and what is acted upon are like, in another unlike; for the unlike is affected, and when it has been affected it is like' (417a19). Aristotle thus modifies the thesis that *like affects like*. He does so by stating that in a way, the sense organ is affected by something unlike it, i.e. the object of perception. Through perceiving, the sense organ becomes like the object of perception. Consider Aristotle's conclusion:

> As we have said, what has the power of sensation is potentially like what the perceived object is actually; that is, while at the beginning of the process of its being acted upon the two interacting factors are dissimilar, at the end the one acted upon is assimilated to the other and is identical in quality with it. (418a4–6)

The thesis *like affects like* thus fails to capture what is happening when we perceive something. According to Aristotle, it is more accurate to say that the organ of perception is affected by something unlike it, and in being affected, the organ of perception becomes like the thing affecting it. Rather than *like affects like*, we might instead say, *unlike becomes like*: what was unlike the object of perception becomes like the object of perception.

We still need to clarify in what way the organ of perception *becomes* the object of perception. The eye does not actually become a burning ball of fire when we perceive the sun; nor does the eye become a wooden and leafy object when we perceive a tree. In his concluding remarks on sense perception, Aristotle explains this notion of becoming:

> Generally, about all perception, we can say that a sense is what has the power of receiving into itself the sensible forms of things without the matter, in the way in which a piece of wax takes on the impress of a signet-ring without the iron or gold; what produces the impression is a signet of bronze or gold, but not *qua* [as] bronze or gold: in a similar way the sense is affected by what is coloured or flavoured or sounding not insofar as each is what it is, but insofar as it is of such and such a sort and according to its form. (424a19–24)

The key idea is that the sense organs are capable of receiving the perceptible form without the matter. The example of the wax and the ring is illuminating: the wax receives the imprint of the ring, i.e. its perceptible form, without receiving the gold or bronze. The wax remains wax, but it has taken on a new form. Likewise with the organs of perception, the organs *become* the object of perception in that the organs take on the perceptible form of the object of perception. When we perceive the sun through the organ of sight, the eye receives the perceptible form of the sun without the matter of the sun. The eye thus does not become the sun as a ball of fire; rather, the eye becomes the sun as the perceptible form of the sun. In a way, the perceptible form of the sun is present in the eye. The sense organs are thus potentially any perceptible form; the sense organs can become anything that we can perceive. Note that throughout this discussion we have been referring to the perceptible form of the object of perception. Perceptible form *(morphe)* is in contrast to the intelligible form *(idea)*. The intelligible form is the form of a thing as it is grasped by the intellect; this includes the plan, design or principle of the thing. The perceptible form is the form of a thing insofar as the form can be perceived; this is the sensible shape, sound, colour or flavour of a thing. The organs of perception thus do not grasp what is intelligible to the intellect; the organs of perception grasp what is sensible.

Aristotle's account of perception also focuses on the way in which perception is a single activity of two things: the object of perception and the organ of perception. Both of these must be present in order for a perception to occur. Having a perception is a moment of activity in which things that existed potentially become actuality. Before it is perceived, the object of perception is only potentially an object of perception; likewise, before it perceives, the organ of perception only potentially perceives. At the moment of activity, both of these potentialities become actualities. Here is Aristotle's description of the two elements in this moment of activity:

> The activity of the sensible object and that of the sense is one and the same activity, and yet the distinction between their being remains. Take as illustration actual sound and actual hearing: a man may have hearing and yet not be hearing, and that which has a sound is not always sounding. But when that which can hear is actively hearing and that which can sound is sounding, then the actual hearing and the actual sound come about at the same time. (425b25–426a1)

There is thus only one activity, though two separate things are involved in the activity. The activity is the having of a perception; but the object of perception and the organ of perception have different roles in the activity. What it is for them to be part of the activity is not the same. Both must be present in order for the activity of perceiving. This presence is short-lived, however; Aristotle states that the hearing and the sounding are simultaneously destroyed and preserved. This helps to illustrate the way in which a perception exists only so long as it lasts. At the moment it is preserved by the organ of sense, it is also destroyed.

A further key point about perception remains. Just as the capacities of soul are ordered in a hierarchy, so too the various forms of perception are ordered in a hierarchy. Of the animals that perceive, all have the sensation of touch (413b5). This is the most basic perceptual capacity that animals have, and nothing perceives without having at least this capacity. Touch can exist apart from the other forms of sense perception. Having this capacity for touch means that the animal is also capable of desiring. Aristotle states:

> If any order of living things has the sensory, it must also have the appetitive; for the appetite is the genus of which desire, passion, and wish are the species; now all animals have one sense at least, viz. touch, and whatever has a sense has the capacity for pleasure and pain and therefore has pleasant and painful objects present to it, and wherever these are present, there is desire, for desire is appetition of what is pleasant. (414b1–6)

Thus with perception comes desire. In perceiving, animals become aware that certain objects external to them are pleasant and some are painful. They desire the pleasant and avoid the painful. Plants, which only have the capacity of nourishment, are not ruled by desire; plants, on this account, do not experience pleasure or pain. The souls of animals, however, are ruled by desire. It is thus appropriate to use the language of desire to describe any animal capable of perceiving.

We thus have in place the general framework of Aristotle's account of perception. Aristotle offers a physiological and causal theory of perception. This account of perception focuses on the way in which objects of perception affect the sense organs. Aristotle maintains that the sense organs are affected in that they take on the perceptible form of the objects of perception. Perception thus involves the sense organs being affected by something unlike them, though through the affection the sense organs become like the object of perception. Aristotle's account also emphasizes the fact that sense organs exist as pure potentiality; the sense organs are only potentiality until some object of perception is presented. The sense organs can potentially become anything that can be perceived. Aristotle's account of perception is valuable not only for its own sake, but also because Aristotle's treatment of the capacity of thought parallels the treatment of perception. In the following section, we shall explore Aristotle's account of the capacity of thought; this is the highest and rarest capacity of soul. It is also the most difficult to comprehend; thus Aristotle treats it in parallel with perception, allowing the capacity that is better understood to illuminate the capacity that is more puzzling.

THOUGHT

Aristotle next turns to the highest and rarest capacity of soul: thought or mind (*nous*). There have been suggestions throughout *On the Soul* that Aristotle regards the capacity of thought differently than the other capacities of soul. All other capacities of soul are the first actualities of certain organs; this explains why the other capacities of soul were found to be inseparable from body. Nutrition, movement and perception are all capacities of some specific material organs. Thought, however, is treated differently. In Book 1.4, Aristotle provides the first inkling that thought must be considered separately from the other capacities of soul:

> But thought seems to be an independent substance implanted within us and to be incapable of being destroyed. If it could be destroyed at all, it would be under the blunting influence of old age. What really happens is, however, exactly parallel to what happens in the case of the sense organs; if the old man could recover the proper kind of eye, he would see just as well as the young man. The incapacity of old age is due to an affection not of the soul but of its vehicle, as occurs in drunkenness or disease. Thus it is that thinking and reflecting decline through the decay of some other inward part and are themselves impassible. Thinking, loving and hating are affections not of thought, but of

that which has thought, so far as it has it. That is why, when this vehicle decays, memory and love cease; they were activities not of thought, but of the composite which has perished; thought is, no doubt, something more divine and impassible. (408b19–30)

The intellect is that by which the soul thinks and supposes (429a21). Aristotle says that the intellect is born into us as a substance and is thus not liable to be destroyed. When a person is no longer able to remember something or to think about something, Aristotle says, it is not thought that has decayed but rather something else within us has decayed. According to this line of reasoning, these affections of soul do not belong to the intellect. Thus when the composite thing dies, the affections of soul are destroyed, but thought is somehow divine and unaffected. Aristotle seems to be saying here that the brain may decay, but that the intellect itself is unaffected; it is born in us as a kind of substance and is not liable to destruction. What is this intellect (*nous*) that is not affected and is divine? It is difficult to understand Aristotle's meaning; nevertheless, the remainder of this section will attempt to clarify Aristotle's conception of intellect.

In *On the Soul* 3.4–5, Aristotle lays out his account of intellect. Thinking is akin to perceiving, but there are important dissimilarities between the two capacities. Unlike the organs of perception, which are only able to perceive those objects suited to the organ, the intellect is capable of thinking all things.[2] The eye can only see what is visible; the ear can only hear what is audible, and so on. But the case of intellect is different; the intellect is able to think all things. Consider Aristotle's argument on this point:

> Therefore, since everything is a possible object of thought, mind in order, as Anaxagoras says, to dominate, that is, to know, must be pure from all admixture; for the co-presence of what is alien to its nature is a hindrance and a block: it follows that it can have no nature of its own, other than that of having a certain capacity. Thus that in the soul which is called thought (by thought I mean that whereby the soul thinks and judges) is, before it thinks, not actually any real thing. For this reason it cannot be reasonably regarded as blended with the body; if so, it would acquire some quality, e.g. warmth or cold, or even have an organ like the sensitive faculty: as it is, it has none. It was a good idea to call the soul 'the place of forms', though this description only holds of the

thinking soul, and even this is the forms only potentially, not actually. (429a18–29)

The main contention of this argument is that because the intellect thinks all things, it must be unmixed with the body; there is thus no organ of thought in the way that there are organs of perception, nutrition and movement. Aristotle likens his view to that of Anaxagoras, but we can understand Aristotle's view without appeal to the Presocratic philosopher Anaxagoras. The basic idea in Aristotle's argument is that if the intellect were mixed with the body, it would take on the characteristics and limitations of the body. Thus if the intellect were mixed with the element water, the intellect would be cold; if the intellect were mixed with the element fire, the intellect would be hot. In being hot or cold, the intellect would be limited to thinking only those things with which it is mixed. But this is clearly not the case, says Aristotle; the intellect thinks all things, and so it cannot be mixed with material elements. This leads Aristotle to the following conclusion about intellect: before the intellect thinks, it is not actually any existing thing. The intellect exists as pure potential. It is potentially any intelligible form.

In the final sentence of the above passage, Aristotle notes the similarity between his own view and the view of Plato and his followers. The Platonists argued that the soul is the place of the Forms; the Forms are actually present in the soul, though we may not be aware of them. For Plato, the Forms must be recovered through a process of recollection. While Aristotle agrees that the soul is the place of forms, he modifies that thesis in two key ways. First, he claims that it is only the part of soul concerned with thought that is the place of forms. The nutritive, locomotive and perceptual capacities of soul have nothing to do with the intelligible forms. Second, Aristotle emphasizes that the forms are in the soul potentially but not actually. Until the soul thinks some intelligible form, the soul is not actually any intelligible form; it is, however, potentially any intelligible form.

Aristotle offers another consideration to show that the intellect is not mixed with the body. He notes that the faculties of perception can be overwhelmed by perceptions that are too intense. After an intense vision, for example, one is less able to see other sights; after a loud sound, one is less able to hear other sounds. The case with intellect is different:

[B]ut in the case of thought, thinking about an object that is highly thinkable renders it more and not less able afterwards to think objects that are less thinkable: the reason is that while the faculty of sensation is dependent upon the body, thought is separable from it. (429b1–5)

Rather than being overwhelmed by intense thoughts, instead the intellect is more able to think lesser thoughts after intense thoughts. Organs that are mixed with matter can be overwhelmed by intense sensations; because the intellect is not so mixed, it does not exhibit the same behaviour as the sense organs. For Aristotle, this is further evidence that the intellect is distinct from the body.

To our modern sensibility this debate about whether the intellect is mixed or unmixed seems misguided. After all, Aristotle is trying to apply a false hypothesis about perception to the case of thought. Given that the hypothesis *like affects like* does not accurately describe perception, it seems unlikely that it could illuminate the case of thought. Aristotle's line of reasoning is thus a reflection of an historical pattern of thought beginning with the Presocratic philosophers. While this discussion about the mixed or unmixed intellect is thus unhelpful, we can at least note the reasoning that compels Aristotle on this point. He seeks to emphasize that the intellect is able to think any intelligible form, while the organs of perception are limited to perceiving only those things appropriate to the organs. But even this point does not seem to entitle Aristotle to the conclusion he seeks to draw regarding the difference between thought and perception. The ultimate result of his reasoning is that the intellect is able to think any intelligible form while perception is able to perceive any perceptible form. While Aristotle's reasoning may be in error on this point, in what follows we shall continue to trace his views regarding the nature of the intellect.

For Aristotle, all indications thus point to the fact that the intellect, or some part of it, is separable from the body and does not need the body to exist. Recall Aristotle's claim that 'some [capacities of soul] may be separable because they are not the actualities of any body at all' (413a4). The unmixed and unaffected intellect, then, is the actuality of no body. This view, however, raises a difficulty for Aristotle. If thinking is at all akin to perceiving, then thinking must involve being affected in some way. Just as the organ of perception takes on the perceptible form of the object of perception, so the intellect takes on the intelligible form of the object of thought (429a16). We have seen the way in which the organ of perception becomes the perceptible form; so it would seem that the intellect in some sense becomes the intelligible form. How can the intellect take on an intelligible form while itself remaining unaffected? In *On the Soul* 3.5, Aristotle introduces a distinction between the active intellect and the passive intellect as an attempt to resolve this difficulty.

Let us first consider Aristotle's remarks on this distinction. As is the case with many of his discussions in *On the Soul*, Aristotle here appeals to analogies to make the problems about soul easier to comprehend. Here is Aristotle's reasoning:

> Since in every class of things, as in nature as a whole, we find two factors involved, a matter which is potentially all the particulars included in the class, a cause which is productive in the sense that it makes them all (the latter standing to the former, as e.g. an art to its material), these distinct elements must likewise be found within the soul. And in fact thought, as we have described it, is what it is by virtue of becoming all things, while there is another which is what it is by virtue of making all things: this is a sort of positive state like light; for in a sense light makes potential colours into actual colours. Thought in this sense of it is separable, impassible, unmixed, since it is in its essential nature activity (for always the active is superior to the passive factor, the originating force to the matter). (430a10–19)

Aristotle begins with a comparison to the whole of nature. In nature, there is an aspect which is the matter and as aspect which is the cause. The matter is potentiality; the matter can potentially become any kind of thing. There is also the cause that produces all kinds of things. In natural substances, this cause is found within the organism; recall that for living organisms, the cause is found in the form. The form or soul provides the internal source of change, i.e. the active cause. The cause and the matter are further related to an art and its material. An art is the cause of producing things, while the matter becomes the things. Consider the example of the art of carpentry. The art is the cause of the production of houses; the material is stones and bricks. The art is productive and active, while the matter is receptive and passive. This distinction in nature between passive matter and active cause is now related to a distinction in the soul.

Given that there is passivity and activity in nature, Aristotle concludes that a similar distinction must be found in the soul's capacity for thought. In nature, matter is passive, receptive and potential; this corresponds to the passive intellect in the soul that becomes all things. In nature, cause is active, productive and actual; this corresponds to the active intellect in the soul that produces all things. The active intellect thus produces all intelligible forms while the passive intellect can potentially become any intelligible form. The active intellect is further characterized as unmixed and unaffected. Thus Aristotle has refined his earlier claim that the intellect must be unaffected and unmixed (429a18–29); only part of this intellect is unaffected and unmixed. The passive intellect is affected and mixed. It becomes the intelligible forms and so is affected; it is also the case that the passive intellect perishes with the body, and so it is mixed with the body (430a25). The active intellect is what is immortal and eternal; its essence is activity, and this cannot cease (430a24). It is not the whole intellect that is immortal; only the active intellect is immortal.

There is another key analogy that Aristotle employs to clarify his rather confusing view about active and passive intellect. He states that the active intellect is like light. Light is the necessary condition that makes potential colours into actual visible colours. Without light, there would be no visible colours. Consider Figure 3 as a representation of Aristotle's analogy:

Faculty	Object	Recipient	Necessary Condition
Sight	Perceptible Form	Eye (Organ)	Light
Intellect	Intelligible Form	Passive Intellect	Active Intellect

Figure 3. A diagram of the analogy between sight and intellect at 430a10–19.

Just as light is the necessary condition for the faculty of sight, so too is the active intellect the necessary condition for the faculty of intellect. In the same way that light makes potential colours into actual visible colours, the active intellect makes potential intelligible forms into actual intelligible forms. Without active intellect, intelligible forms would not be intelligible at all, just as without light, visible colours would not be visible at all. The passive recipient corresponding to the matter is the passive intellect; the passive intellect is like the eye, which is the organ of sight. The passive intellect is thus the matter for the faculty of intellect; it is the organ that receives and becomes the intelligible forms.

It seems natural to identify the passive intellect with the brain, but it is not clear how to identify the active intellect. The passive intellect is liable to decay, just as the organs of perception are liable to decay. If our memory fails or we are unable to think certain thoughts, it is the decay of the material organ that is to blame. As Aristotle says, thought itself, i.e. active intellect, does not decay and is unaffected; thought, he says, is born in us as a kind of substance (408b19, 24). A further difficulty arises in interpreting Aristotle's conception of active intellect. Light, it will be noted, is not in the eye or in the animal; light is rather the medium outside of the animal that enables perception to occur. Might it be possible that active intellect is outside of the body in the way that light is outside of the body? There is some evidence to suggest that Aristotle does not intend active intellect to be understood as something from without. He states, 'thought seems to be an independent substance implanted within us and to be incapable of being destroyed' (408b19). It seems clear that the sense of intellect Aristotle has in mind here is active intellect; we have seen already how passive intellect is liable to destruction. Active intellect, then, is not something outside of us, but is rather within us as a kind of substance that is not destroyed. The illumination, so to speak, of intelligible forms, does not depend upon something outside of us; rather, the illuminating force is within us. This suggests a point at which the analogy between light and active intellect breaks down; whereas light is an external medium, Aristotle seems to understand active intellect as an internal illuminator of intelligible forms. Following this line of reasoning, there is some aspect of intellect within us that is immortal; passive intellect dies with the body, but active intellect lives on.

Students of Plato may note echoes of Plato's sun analogy from the *Republic* in Aristotle's treatment of active intellect.[3] In that famous analogy, Plato likens the Form of the Good to the sun; it is the form that makes all other forms intelligible. In the way that the sun illuminates perceptible objects, the Form of the Good illuminates intelligible objects. This seems very similar to Aristotle's analogy between light and the active intellect: just as light makes perceptible forms visible, the active intellect makes intelligible forms intelligible. I am not here suggesting that Aristotle and Plato are in complete agreement on matters of the intellect. Rather, it is interesting to note that both Plato and Aristotle treat the intelligible on analogy with the perceptible. Both Plato and Aristotle thus seem to hold that there must be some illuminating force in the realm of the intelligible, just as there is an illuminating force in the realm of the perceptible. This issue is extraordinarily difficult to describe precisely and clearly; both Aristotle and Plato found the issue difficult enough that they resorted to argument by analogy as a way to make their meaning clear. They seem to have reached the boundary of what is comprehensible to us, and so appeal to analogy is the only available means to state their views. Both Plato and Aristotle would seem to be in agreement on certain key points: there is some eternal aspect of intellect (*nous*) that is active and productive and is the means by which any intelligible form is thinkable. This aspect of intellect is the necessary condition for any thinking at all. Beyond these points, however, it is difficult to state their views with precision and certainty.

The immortality of the intellect coheres well with Plato's general views about the soul and the forms. A dualist like Plato would naturally maintain that the soul is a separable substance that can and must live on after its association with the body. For Aristotle, however, the consistency of his account of the soul seems threatened by his treatment of the intellect. We have seen how Aristotle's hylemorphic theory of natural substances conceives of soul as the actuality of a natural body. The soul is not a separate entity within the body; the soul is just the structure, plan and capacities of a potentially living natural body. There is only one thing – the living natural substance – that can be considered through two aspects, i.e. its matter and its soul. Whereas Plato proposes a dualism of substances, Aristotle proposes a dualism of aspects; there are material and formal aspects to living things, but these material and formal aspects do not exist as separable and self-subsistent substances. Aristotle's account of intellect, however, seems to suggest that there is one part of the soul that is not the actuality of any body or natural organ. Thus the hylemorphic approach holds for all the capacities of soul except for the active intellect; even the passive intellect seems to adhere to the hylemorphic model. We are thus faced with a challenge in reconstructing Aristotle's account of the soul: we need to understand what motivated Aristotle to deviate from the hylemorphic model in the case of active intellect. It seems that Aristotle treats the active intellect as an indwelling substance in the living thing; this sounds very much like the substance dualist theories of the soul.

Aristotle's account of the soul, and in particular his account of intellect, has perplexed commentators ever since it was written. We are not here able to resolve this inconsistency that seems present in his account of the soul, but we can indicate some reasons why the intellect receives a different treatment. Though Aristotle treats intellect in parallel with perception, he seems to have been impressed by three pivotal distinctions between the cases of thought and perception. First, intellect is able to think all intelligible forms, whereas the organs of perception are only able to perceive perceptible forms appropriate to the organs: sight can only see the visible, hearing can only hear the audible, and so on. The intellect is not like this: all intelligible forms are capable of being thought by the intellect. The organs of perception are mixed with material elements; the organs of perception are composed of mixtures of earth, air, water or fire. This mixing with material elements in some sense constrains what the organ of perception can perceive or *become*. Since the intellect is not limited in this way, Aristotle seems to conclude that the intellect must not have a material component; it must be, he says, unmixed. We have already noted that this distinction is not as compelling to us as it seems to have been to Aristotle.

The second difference between the faculties of perception and thought concerns the spontaneity of the intellect. Aristotle observes:

> Actual sensation corresponds to the stage of the exercise of knowledge. But between the two cases compared there is a difference; the objects that excite the sensory powers to activity, the seen, the heard, &c., are outside. The ground of this difference is that what actual sensation apprehends is individuals, while what knowledge apprehends is universals, and these are in a sense within the soul itself. That is why a man can think what he wants to but his sensation does not depend upon himself – a sensible object must be there. (417b19–25)

This passage concludes that the intellect is spontaneous while perception is dependent. For a perception to occur there must be an external object; this is why we cannot choose to perceive whatever we wish at any given moment. Yet matters are different with intellect; we are able to think whatever we wish whenever we want. This spontaneous activity of the intellect is not absolute, however; we can only conceive of universals after being exposed to particulars. Recall the discussion from *Posterior Analytics* in which Aristotle tries to show how our understanding of universal terms derives from experience of particulars.[4] Once we have achieved knowledge of universals, however, we are able to think those universals whenever we wish. Intellect is thus unmixed and spontaneous. In order for this spontaneity to exist, there must be intellect whose essence is activity. If the essence of something is activity, then that activity cannot cease. Hence we have the unmixed intellect whose essence is activity. This is the source of all universals, i.e. all intelligible forms.

A third reason why Aristotle treats intellect differently than perception concerns the striving of natural substances for immortality. Each natural substance reproduces as a way of participating in the immortal species. In addition, as human beings, we participate in the activity of thought. In participating in thinking, we are participating in something divine and immortal; thought itself cannot be destroyed. Human contemplation reflects a striving for immortality. We shall see this argument advanced in our discussion of the *Nicomachean Ethics*, in which Aristotle argues that the highest form of human life is the contemplative life.[5] Thought is thus unmixed, spontaneous and immortal; for all these reasons it is a fundamentally different kind of activity from perceiving. It must be granted that the divinity of intellect is an undefended assumption in Aristotle's overall argument; but there can be no mistaking that he considers intellect in this way. On the whole, however, Aristotle's attempts to draw a distinction between perception and thought do not seem compelling; his attempts to draw a distinction certainly do not seem to support his apparent acceptance of a substance dualist view in the case of thought. Had Aristotle remained consistent with his hylemorphic view and extended it to the case of thought, his theory would retain consistency and would have several advantages as an account of soul and life. As it is, his theory is torn between two ways of considering the soul. To be charitable to Aristotle, we should keep in mind the extraordinary nature of thought; for Aristotle, it is truly incredible how thinking ever comes about. In order for thinking to come about, he argues that there must be a part of the soul that is immaterial, active and immortal.

Though there are a number of difficult unresolved issues in Aristotle's account of the soul, it must still be admitted that *On the*

Soul is an absolutely remarkable work of philosophy and science. Aristotle sets out to explain that most wondrous phenomenon of the natural world – life. In so doing, he proposes an account of the soul that identifies it with the first actuality of a body with organs; thus the soul is a set of capacities. When we say that something is alive, then, we are saying that it has certain powers or capacities; living things can do things that non-living things cannot do. The capacities of living things include nutrition, reproduction, locomotion, perception and thought. Aristotle's account of the soul also attempts to explain how living things do the things that they do; thus much of *On the Soul* is concerned with physiological and causal explanations of the various capacities of soul. This discussion of soul will prove useful for the topic of the last chapter: success or flourishing (*eudaimonia*). All living things ultimately strive for the flourishing that is appropriate to their kind of soul. Our next topic will thus be the uniquely human flourishing that is the cornerstone of Aristotle's ethics.

CHAPTER 5

SUCCESS (*EUDAIMONIA*)

Aristotle's ethical writings have been profoundly influential in both the ancient and modern worlds. In contemporary scholarship, Aristotle's ethics is the most active and lively field of Aristotelian studies. Many students of Aristotle begin by studying his ethics or they study only his ethical writings. The structure of this book suggests that such an approach is deeply misguided. Aristotle's ethical writings are best understood as the culmination of his philosophical and scientific thought. His writings in metaphysics, natural science and the soul all underpin his ethics; to approach his ethics we must appreciate the metaphysical, natural and psychological foundations upon which his ethics depends.

The central concept in Aristotle's ethics is *eudaimonia*. This Greek term originally meant *to be favoured by the gods* or *to be blessed by the gods*. By Aristotle's time, the religious significance of this term had faded, but it was still employed to describe the success that a human being can achieve in his or her life. Instead of the religious connotations, *eudaimonia* came to be understood as the success that a human being secures through his or her own actions and choices. Rather than being conferred upon us by the gods, *eudaimonia* is something of our own making. The term *eudaimonia* can be rendered as *happiness*, *success* or *flourishing*. For Aristotle, ethics is a practical science; its aim is to achieve success through action. Thus Aristotle sets out to explain the success or flourishing which human beings can achieve through action. In a crucial sense, then, Aristotle is offering a guide for how to plan our lives such that they will turn out to be a success. All human beings seek to achieve success in their lives, but success is a rare and exceptional thing. Though we think success is the crowning achievement of a lifetime, there is dispute about what a successful life involves and how to attain it.

In the *Nicomachean Ethics*, Aristotle develops a reflective understanding of success or flourishing for human beings. We shall consider his reasoning regarding success in the section of this chapter entitled 'The Chief and Final Good'. Aristotle provides two competing accounts of success that both draw heavily upon his findings in *On the Soul*. Once he has settled on these accounts of success, he develops a theory of the virtues to enable us to secure this success for ourselves. Aristotle's account of *eudaimonia* is notable for its subtlety and richness, and his theory of the virtues shines as an astounding philosophical triumph. Aristotle argues that we can achieve success in our lives not by following any rules or moral laws, but rather by cultivating a set of virtues of character and virtues of intellect. We achieve success by developing ourselves into a certain kind of person. These virtues of character include courage, justice, self-control, good temper, friendliness, honesty and so on. By cultivating these virtues of character, and by developing the intellectual virtue of practical wisdom, we put ourselves in a position to act well in any given situation. Once again, there are no prescribed ethical rules or moral laws for living a successful life. The best we can do is to develop virtues of character and intellect and apply those virtues through action in the various situations that we face in our lives.

It may be objected at this point that Aristotle's ethics is not moral philosophy at all. Conventional moral theory, as it is commonly understood, concerns our duties and obligations towards others or towards the moral law. The two main representatives of conventional moral theory are deontology and utilitarianism. Moral philosophy involves the articulation of rules and principles for conduct. Conventional moral philosophy also concerns questions of what is *right*. Such moral theories do not concern themselves with being successful; one can be successful and still morally corrupt. Hence the key to deontology and utilitarianism is doing what is right, not merely succeeding. Further, the focus of deontological and utilitarian theories is on individual actions and whether or not such actions are morally permissible. These moral theories thus provide accounts of what makes individual actions permissible or impermissible. Conventional moral theories largely ignore issues of character; regardless of one's character, certain actions are permissible and certain actions are impermissible.

Aristotle, however, does not seem to be concerned with this conception of moral philosophy. Nowhere does he discuss duty or obligation; nor does he describe moral rules or principles. Indeed, he seems highly sceptical of the possibility of moral rules or principles. Aristotle's ethics focuses primarily on individual *character* rather than individual *actions*; the distinction is subtle but crucial. Aristotle is interested in individual actions in a secondary way; individual actions are important only insofar as they produce a virtuous character. Further, Aristotle's ethics is crucially self-centred rather than other-directed; each agent should seek what is good *for her*, not for others. Many theories in moral philosophy are concerned with our duty to others, but this is not Aristotle's approach. The concept of altruism, which is so prominent in conventional ethical theories, is absent in Aristotle's virtue ethics. This is not to say that the lives of others are irrelevant to our own success and flourishing; on the contrary, for each of us to live well, we need friends and family with whom to share our success. We do not, however, achieve success for them; we achieve it for ourselves. In these basic and foundational respects, then, Aristotle's ethical project diverges from other conventional ethical theories.

Aristotle's ethics is much more concerned with providing a practical guideline for how to achieve human flourishing. Attending to the key Greek terms can help to illuminate Aristotle's conception of ethics. The Greek word for *ethics* (*ethike*) is closely related to the word for *character* (*ethos*). Thus rather than approaching ethics in the sense of *moral* philosophy, Aristotle approaches ethics as the science of human character. We develop excellences of character not because they are *morally right*, but because they enable us to flourish. His investigation will thus enable us to develop the excellences of character that are a core element in human happiness. This approach to ethics is grounded in Aristotle's view that all natural substances can achieve a flourishing that is appropriate to them; he also takes it as a given that flourishing is better than infirmity. We do not say that it is morally right for a plant to flourish; rather, we say that flourishing is what a plant naturally aspires to for its own sake. Likewise with human beings, it is not morally right for us to flourish; rather, flourishing is what we naturally aspire to for our own sake. It is not our duty or obligation to become happy or successful; we naturally aspire to happiness and success. Rather than being concerned with doing what is right, Aristotle is concerned with enabling us to live well. To be sure, living well serves the supreme good in the whole of nature. Note, however, that what is *naturally good* is not the same as what is *morally right*. The former concept is the driving force in Aristotle's ethics, while the latter concept guides Kantian ethics, utilitarian ethics and many forms of Christian ethics.

Many conventional moral philosophers will find the above explanation of Aristotle's approach unsatisfactory. It seems that the terms *ethics* and *moral philosophy* have radically different meanings under conventional moral theory and virtue theory. From this discussion, it seems apparent that conventional moral theory and virtue theory are theories that explain different kinds of phenomena. Some philosophers have maintained that there cannot be any real disagreement between conventional moral theory and virtue theory because the theories concern different things. The theories use some of the same terminology, but the terminology is understood in very different ways. Conventional moral theory concerns what is right, while virtue theory concerns what will lead to success. As I hope to demonstrate in the following, Aristotle's focus on success does not allow us to pursue simply any course of action. There are still limits to what we can do, though these limits are practical rather than moral. For Aristotle, we should avoid certain actions not because they are morally wrong, but because they harm our chances for success. This conflict between conventional moral theory and virtue ethics is perhaps one of the most intractable in all of philosophy.[1] At stake is the very conception of what the normative philosophy of human behaviour should be. The best way to approach the issue is to investigate each of these approaches in depth; we shall here investigate virtue theory as Aristotle develops it.

Aristotle's theory of *eudaimonia* and his account of virtues of character and intellect are the cornerstones of his ethical theory. Before we can approach these topics, however, there are several key prefatory issues to explore. The following section serves as a preface to the rest of Aristotle's ethical thought.

THE PRACTICAL SCIENCE OF ETHICS

Aristotle's ethics is the only practical science treated in this book. Recall that Aristotle classifies all sciences according to their aims: theoretical sciences aim at understanding, practical sciences aim at action, and productive sciences aim at making some useful or beautiful object.[2] Ethics and politics are both practical sciences; the aim of these sciences is to achieve the good for human beings through fine and noble actions. Politics takes as its object of inquiry the nation or city-state (*polis*), while ethics takes as its object of inquiry human character (*ethos*). Politics thus studies human societies while ethics studies human individuals. Aristotle suggests that politics is the master practical science and that ethics is subordinate to politics (1094b1–11). Ethics studies how to achieve the good for an individual person, while politics studies how to achieve the good for a nation: 'for though it is worth while to attain the end merely for one man, it is finer and more godlike to attain it for a nation or for city-states' (1094b9–10). Because the aim of politics is loftier than that of ethics, Aristotle regards politics as the authoritative practical science.

Nevertheless, ethics is crucial to politics, for the state is composed of individual human beings. Thus the constitution and the legislators of a state will be concerned with matters of ethics; for example, how the young are raised is a matter of vital importance for the well-being of the state. In the final chapter of the final book (10.9) of the *Nicomachean Ethics*, Aristotle transitions from the study of ethics to the study of politics. He argues that it is a concern for legislators how the young are nurtured, what habits they develop, and what occupations they pursue (1180a1–12). All of these are matters that should be set in law. In order for the state to benefit, the state must take an interest in the nurturing of its individual citizens. In so doing, the state can encourage through legislation our aspiration to success. Thus while we study ethics to understand the good achievable for a single human being, our goal is ultimately to achieve this good for a nation.

Ethics and politics are both practical sciences, and Aristotle draws the contrast between practical and theoretical sciences early in the *Nicomachean Ethics*:

> Since, then, the present inquiry does not aim at theoretical knowledge like the others (for we are inquiring not in order to know what excellence is, but in order to become good, since otherwise our inquiry would have been of no use), we must examine the nature of actions, namely how we ought to do them. (1103b26–30)[3]

The aim of our inquiry, then, is to become good human beings. We do not merely want to understand what a good human life is; we want to achieve it for ourselves. For Aristotle, we achieve *eudaimonia* by performing fine and noble actions. Thus locating ethics and politics as practical sciences reveals one of Aristotle's key insights about human life: human life is an activity. We achieve a happy and flourishing life through our actions.

An illustration may help to clarify Aristotle's notion of human life as an activity. As human beings, we can live either poorly or well; Aristotle takes it as a given that human beings should aspire to live well. The operative Greek term is *arête*, which can be translated as *excellence* or *virtue*. The term *arête* is used not only to define human activities, but also the activities of artefacts and natural objects. It is appropriate to speak, for example, of the *arête* of a knife. The essence or form of a knife is its capacity to cut; the excellence of a knife is its ability to cut well. In order to be an excellent knife, it must be made of the appropriate materials and it must also be properly cared for and sharpened. The materials and care can be understood as the preconditions for an excellent knife. The excellence of a knife, however, is not determined by these preconditions; rather, the excellence of a knife is determined by how the knife performs when it is called upon to cut. Its excellence, then, is determined by how well it performs its characteristic activity. We can imagine a knife that is made of the proper materials and is cared for properly, and yet it does not cut well; we would not regard such a knife as excellent.

A similar line of reasoning obtains for human excellence. Just as a knife has a characteristic activity, so also do human beings. The characteristic activity of human beings is to act using reason. Like plants, we nourish ourselves and reproduce. Like animals, we perceive and desire. Whereas animals simply act to satisfy their desires, human beings use their reason to make choices in order to satisfy their desires (1097b30–1098a17). This pattern of desire and choice is the essence of human activity. We deliberate and calculate concerning how best to meet our desires. A person is thus excellent insofar as they act successfully using their reason to satisfy their desires. Though we desire to feel pleasure and avoid pain, there are numerous other desires that drive human beings. As the first line of the *Metaphysics* tells us, 'all human beings by nature desire to know' (980a20). Human beings also desire friendship and love (*philia*). We can further desire wealth, power and honour. We can, of course, also desire things that are harmful to us. Aristotle's ethics will thus explain what kinds of things are appropriate to desire; things that contribute to human flourishing should be desired, while things that are harmful to human flourishing should be avoided. We must thus desire the right kinds of things and use our reason well to satisfy those desires. A human being who is consistently able to act well with respect to the right kinds of desires achieves excellence or virtue.

Implicit in the above remarks about desire and choice is that all of our actions aim at something we think is good for us. This point is established in the first lines of the *Nicomachean Ethics*: 'Every art and every inquiry, and similarly every action and choice, is thought to aim at some good; and for this reason the good has rightly been declared to be that at which all things aim' (1094a1–3). Aristotle's teleology is thus at the forefront of his ethical theory. The actions and choices of human beings aim at some good; the good at which we aim is thus an end or goal (*telos*). There are two ways in which this thesis can be understood, and it is likely that Aristotle intends both meanings. First, this claim can be understood as a psychological law: for any human being, all of her actions and choices aim at what she thinks is good for her. This psychological law is true whether or not the human being is conscious that she is acting for some good; this law also holds even if the human being cannot articulate her goals for action. Once again, we see how for Aristotle intention is not the only mark of goal-directed behaviour. Even if we are not aware of our goals or cannot articulate our goals, it is still the case that every action and every choice aims at some goal.

Aristotle's view can also be interpreted as normative ethical advice: all human actions and choices *should* aim at what is good for human beings. On this interpretation, Aristotle would seek to clarify what are the right goods at which human beings should aim and what are the right means by which we can achieve those goods. As a matter of psychological law, then, human beings are such that their actions and choices aim at some end (*telos*) that is good for them. In order to achieve human excellence, Aristotle says, we should seek to determine what is good for human beings, i.e. at what good(s) we should aim. Aristotle uses a metaphor regarding archers and their targets: just as archers are more likely to hit their target if they can see it and aim at it, so also are human beings more likely to hit their target, i.e. the good, if they know what it is (1094a24). One of the main goals of Aristotle's ethics, then, is to provide us with the target at which our actions should aim. This involves becoming conscious of our aims and being able to articulate our aims. Aristotle challenges us to harness the laws of our own psychology to achieve the good for us. We cannot help but seek what is good for us, so at the very least we should develop a reflective understanding of what is good for us and how we can attain it. Characterizing this final and chief good is the topic of the next section of this chapter. Once we know what this final and chief good is, we will then turn to the means by which we can achieve this good.

Aristotle also discusses the precision and exactness that we should aspire to in the practical science of ethics.[4] All sciences proceed from axioms by means of demonstration, but not all sciences achieve the same degree of precision and exactness. In order to undertake this inquiry into ethics, we must understand what level of precision is appropriate to ethics. Consider Aristotle's remarks on this issue:

> Our discussion will be adequate if it has as much clearness as the subject-matter admits of; for precision is not to be sought for alike in all discussions, any more than in all the products of the crafts. Now fine and just actions, which political science investigates, exhibit much variety and fluctuation, so that they may be thought to exist only by convention, and not by nature. And goods also exhibit a similar fluctuation because they bring harm to many people; for before now men have been undone by reason of their wealth, and others by reason of their courage. We must be content, then, in speaking of such subjects and with such premises to indicate the truth roughly and in outline, and in speaking about things which are only for the most part true and with premises of the same kind to reach conclusions that are no better. In the same spirit, therefore, should each of our statements be *received*; for it is the mark of an educated man to look for precision in each class of things just so far as the nature of the subject admits: it is evidently equally foolish to accept probable reasoning from a mathematician and to demand from a rhetorician demonstrative proofs. (1094b12–26)

Later in the *Nicomachean Ethics*, Aristotle reinforces this theme with a helpful analogy:

And we must also remember what has been said before, and not look for precision in all things alike, but in each class of things such as accords with the subject-matter, and so much as is appropriate to the inquiry. For a carpenter and a geometer look for right angles in different ways; the former does so in so far as the right angle is useful for his work, while the latter inquires what it is or what sort of thing it is; for he is a spectator of the truth. (1098a25–31)

There are two key points developed in the above passages. First, ethics is the study of fine and noble actions and the goods at which those actions aim. Actions and goods, however, exhibit much variety and fluctuation. Not all fine actions are alike, nor are all goods alike. Actions and goods depend to a large extent upon the circumstances in which an agent finds himself. Aristotle observes that many people have been undone by their courage or their pursuit of wealth. It is not the case, then, that wealth is always a good; in some cases, it can be harmful or destructive. What is good is thus not fixed; goods are instead liable to fluctuation. This variety and fluctuation of actions and goods has an important consequence for the study of ethics: our premises and conclusions must be received as rough outlines of the truth. There will always be possible counter-examples in which wealth or courage are harmful, and likewise with all other goods; we should thus not demand universal and exceptionless rules in this science. There are no precise and exact demonstrations in ethics; the best we can do is sketch the truth roughly and in outline. This is due to the nature of the subject matter.

The above passages also highlight the distinction between theoretical understanding and practical utility. Consider Aristotle's example concerning the way that a carpenter and a geometer study right angles: the carpenter is concerned with utility, i.e. how well an angle serves the goal of building, while the geometer is a 'spectator of the truth'. The carpenter is interested in right angles insofar as they further his goals for building; a geometer has no end in mind other than pure understanding. In ethics, we are not merely spectators of the truth; rather, we are living human beings who are trying to achieve the good in our own lives. Thus we seek ethical knowledge for its usefulness in helping us to achieve our goals. In ethics we seek the degree of precision that is appropriate to the subject matter as well as the precision that enables us to use this ethical knowledge to achieve human flourishing. We might conclude that because ethics helps us to live well, it should be regarded more highly than the theoretical sciences, which aim only at understanding. This, however, is not Aristotle's view. Aristotle is adamant that there is no pursuit nobler than that of understanding alone. The utility of the practical and productive sciences makes them subordinate to the sciences that aim at understanding. In general, Aristotle values more highly those sciences that arise through leisure and that do not serve any practical or productive end.

Aristotle adds a further point of clarification regarding the precision that we can expect in ethics. Consider:

> [M]atters concerned with conduct and questions of what is good for us have no fixity, any more than matters of health. The general account being of this nature, the account of particular cases is yet more lacking in exactness; for they do not fall under any art or set of precepts, but the agents themselves must in each case consider what is appropriate to the occasion, as happens also in the art of medicine or of navigation. (1104a5–9)

In this passage, Aristotle explicitly rejects the idea that particular cases fall under a set of rules or precepts. Rather, he states that individuals must in each particular case decide what is appropriate. The comparison with medicine is helpful. Medicine aims at health, but matters of health lack fixity just as matters of ethics. Something that may produce health in many cases might produce harm in one particular case; it is up to the doctor to evaluate each particular case and to decide what is appropriate. In medicine and in ethics, there are no universal and exceptionless rules. In ethics, there are no rules such as *always tell the truth* or *never kill a human being*. There may be cases in which the best thing to do is to lie or to kill; it is up to the agent in each particular case to determine what course of action is best. Certainly ethics would be simpler if we could all just follow a set of rules; but living well, for Aristotle, is vastly more complicated than simply following a set of rules. Likewise, practising medicine is not just a matter of following rules. Rules cannot cover every possible scenario; rules can come into conflict with each other; further, there is no one set of rules that all people can agree upon. The best that we can do, in ethics and in medicine, is to develop our judgement, experience and character such that we can decide what course of action is best in any given situation.

This section on the practical science of ethics serves as a preface to Aristotle's ethical thought. Our primary source material for these prefatory issues is the *Nicomachean Ethics* 1.1–3. These prefatory issues are crucial for understanding Aristotle's ethical project. We now understand the aim and objects of the science of ethics. Ethics studies what is good for human beings; this is the object of ethics. Ethics aims at enabling us to become good. In order to enable us to become good, ethics studies what is good for human beings and the means by which we can achieve what is good for us. For Aristotle, the good is achieved through action; in ethics we are studying the kinds of fine and noble actions that enable one to achieve human flourishing. In the next section of this chapter, we will investigate the chief and final good of human life: *eudaimonia*. This is the target at which our actions should aim. We will also investigate the means by which we can hit this target. According to Aristotle, we hit this target by cultivating our moral and intellectual virtues (*arête*).

THE CHIEF AND FINAL GOOD FOR HUMAN BEINGS

In the *Nicomachean Ethics* 1.7 Aristotle gives an account of the end at which all our actions aim. We have stated in the preceding that happiness, success or flourishing (*eudaimonia*) is the end of all that we do; in this section, we shall here investigate the arguments by which Aristotle arrives at this conclusion. In addition, we shall attempt to give a description of a flourishing life; we will be able to hit our target more readily if we know what our target is. Thus Aristotle outlines the highest excellence attainable by action for human beings. Also in this section, we shall treat the two competing versions of the good life presented by Aristotle: the life of practical success and the life of contemplation.

Aristotle begins by emphasizing that the end that we are seeking must be achievable by action (1096b34, 1097a24). This reinforces the point that we are dealing with a practical science. This point also rules out purely theoretical notions of the good; the only good that is relevant to Aristotle's ethics is the good achievable through action. Aristotle is highly critical of theoretical conceptions of the good espoused by Plato and his followers. Aristotle seeks, then, 'the end for all that we do' (1097a22). This suggests that all of our actions are directed towards one highest good. If we are to apply Aristotle's notion of the four causes or explanations, the highest good at which all our actions aim is the final cause. Recall that Aristotle describes the final cause as *the cause for the sake of which*. In this context, the material cause is the body of the human being; the formal cause is the soul of the human being. The efficient cause is the agent who takes action. The final cause is *the cause for the sake of which*, i.e. the end or goal sought through the action. Why does this human being perform action X? Aristotle's reply: in order to become happy or successful. All actions that we do contribute to achieving this final cause; this final cause is the reason why we do anything. It is the chief and final good. Note how this conception of the goal of human life differs from the goals of action as stated by conventional moral theories. For deontological or utilitarian theories, the goal of action is doing what is *right*, either by upholding the moral law or by maximizing utility. Aristotle's virtue ethics does not aim at what is right; his ethics aims instead at success. This is a basic and foundational difference between conventional ethical theories and virtue ethics.

Aristotle describes the chief and final good as complete and self-sufficient. He states, 'we call complete without qualification that which is always desirable in itself and never for the sake of something else' (1097a33–35). Aristotle defines as self-sufficient 'that which when isolated makes life desirable and lacking in nothing' (1097b15). The chief and final good we are seeking is therefore something desirable in itself and never for the sake of something else. This means that we pursue the chief and final good for its own sake; we never pursue the chief and final good as a means to some other good. The chief and final good also lacks nothing; it cannot be enhanced by the addition of anything else. Once you have this chief and final good, you have all that you could want. Aristotle concludes that success is thought to be something of this sort. All that we do we do for the sake of attaining success. If we pursue wealth or pleasure, we do so because we believe these things will ultimately contribute to our success. But wealth alone is not a complete and self-sufficient good; nor is pleasure alone complete and self-sufficient. We always desire success for its own sake and not for the sake of something else. When we have achieved success, we think that our lives are lacking in nothing; our lives possess all that we could hope for. Aristotle adds that success must be manifest 'in a complete life' (1098a18). It should be clear by now that the kind of happiness Aristotle is here discussing is not a fleeting or momentary state; it is rather a stable state that is 'something of one's own and not easily taken from one' (1095b25).

This is one reason why many translators opt to render *eudaimonia* as *flourishing* or *success* rather than *happiness*; in English, *happiness* can mean a fleeting or momentary state of satisfaction or pleasure. This is clearly not what Aristotle means by *eudaimonia*. Thus we should keep in mind that the chief and final good is a stable and lasting state of flourishing that is complete and self-sufficient and that endures for a complete life.

Aristotle rightly observes, however, that regarding success as the chief and final good is to some extent an unhelpful and uninteresting thesis. Everyone would agree that we all strive for success; Aristotle's discussion has thus revealed little more than what the average person in the street would claim. Aristotle attempts to clarify further what is meant by success or flourishing. There is a kind of flourishing appropriate to each kind of living thing. We know what it means for a plant or an animal to flourish; the question now is what human flourishing involves. Aristotle approaches this issue by considering what is the function or purpose (*ergon*) of human beings (1097b22–1098a17). For all things, whether natural object or artefact, there is some activity characteristic of that thing. Aristotle seeks the characteristic activity of human beings by considering what is peculiar to human beings among all natural substances. The vegetative life of nourishment, growth and reproduction cannot be the peculiar human function, for we share these capacities with plants. Nor can the life of perception and desire be the human function, for we share these capacities with animals. What distinguishes human beings from all other natural substances is that we live according to a rational principle in the soul. We deliberate and calculate regarding how to satisfy our desires. Since any object can perform its characteristic activity poorly or well, Aristotle concludes that the chief and final good for human beings is a rational activity of the soul in conformity with excellence (*arête*). This is what is meant by success, happiness or flourishing.

Aristotle further refines this conception of flourishing. He argues that the capacities of nourishment, growth and reproduction have no share in reason and thus no share in human excellence (1102b1–11). These capacities are part of the irrational element in the soul. As further evidence that these capacities do not share in human excellence, Aristotle notes that no one is praised or blamed for their nourishment, growth or reproduction. These capacities do not involve reason; nor do these capacities yield to or listen to reason. There is another part of the irrational element in the soul that does share in the rational principle (1102b12–1103a3). For Aristotle, with perception of pleasure and pain comes the desire to feel pleasure and avoid pain. The desiring element in us can share in the rational principle because our desiring element can either obey reason or resist reason. We are praised, Aristotle notes, for having a desiring element that obeys reason and we are blamed for having a desiring element that resists reason. If the irrational desiring element can share in reason, then it is also possible to achieve excellence with respect to this desiring element. Indeed, for Aristotle, a person achieves excellence or virtue insofar as that person uses reason to satisfy desires that contribute to human flourishing. A virtuous person is one who is able to effectively and consistently make choices that lead to the fulfilment of his or her desires.

Let us take this opportunity to flesh out more fully the flourishing life that is achievable by action. Aristotle presents two conceptions of the flourishing life. In Book 1 of *Nicomachean Ethics*, he develops what we shall call the comprehensive account of the good life; this account requires the flourishing of all the capacities of the soul. In Book 10 of *Nicomachean Ethics*, Aristotle presents a strictly contemplative account of the flourishing life. In what follows, we shall explore both of these conceptions of *eudaimonia*; we shall also consider why Aristotle presents these two different conceptions. It is possible to understand these two conceptions in the light of Aristotle's account of the human soul in *On the Soul*.

The comprehensive account of *eudaimonia* involves practical success at the fulfilment of the full range of human capacities. We can determine what this life is like by examining the lives of those people whom we credit with achieving *eudaimonia*. This life of practical success is achievable by action, so if we wish to understand it better, we would do well to examine the lives of those who have achieved such success in their own lives. Once again, we see how for Aristotle the good life is not some theoretical ideal; rather, it is the life achievable, and achieved, by action. Aristotle emphasizes that those who act well are the ones who achieve the good life; he shows this by analogy with athletic competition:

> And as in the Olympic Games it is not the most beautiful and the strongest that are crowned but those who compete (for it is some of these that are victorious), so those who act rightly win the noble and good things in life. (1099a2–5)

The good life is therefore not defined by inactivity or possession; it is rather something achieved by acting well. Simply being good is not sufficient; one must translate one's goodness into practical success. As with the Olympic analogy, simply being beautiful or strong is not enough; one must get out there and compete. Thus the good life is something that we make for ourselves; it is not something merely given to us through fortune or luck. Aristotle rightly observes that we do not praise or blame people for misfortunes due to chance or luck; we do, however, praise or blame them for the voluntary choices they make regarding their lives.

The comprehensive account of *eudaimonia* thus requires that a person achieve the full range of human flourishing through his or her own actions and choices. There are two main types of goods that are required for this flourishing: goods of the soul and external goods. The parts of the soul that can share in excellence are perception, which includes desire, and reason. We must cultivate the excellences or virtues of character that enable us to fulfil these elements in our souls. The flourishing person will thus exhibit the virtues of courage, temperance or moderation, justice, good temper, generosity and so on. We shall discuss the details of Aristotle's theory of the virtues in the next section of this chapter; at this point we will consider the entirety of one's character. For the desiring element in us to flourish, it must be the case that we desire the right kinds of things and that these desires are satisfied. This does not mean that we should simply give ourselves over to every desire that we have; Aristotle is clear that such a life of pure pleasure is more suitable for beasts than for human beings. Yet Aristotle also maintains that the flourishing life is pleasant to the person who has it (1099a5). A person who is in a state of suffering is not flourishing; the flourishing person has the right kinds of desires and she uses her reason well to satisfy those desires. Aristotle holds that rather than settling for a life of the basest pleasures, we should aspire to enjoy the most refined pleasures in life. These refined pleasures include the genuine love and friendship (*philia*) of others. We achieve a refined pleasure in our dealings with other human beings. For Aristotle, human beings are political and social animals; the good life for us, then, is not a life of isolation. Rather, the good life involves social activity. Successful political activity, then, is source of pleasure. Aristotle also states that flourishing involves attaining personal independence. Anyone who has to work for a living is beholden to a superior; someone who is truly successful would ensure that they are beholden to no one but themselves. We also need to satisfy the rational element in the soul. This means that we must use our practical reason successfully to achieve the ends that we set for ourselves. This also involves creating a life of sufficient leisure that we can give ourselves over to the rewards of philosophical contemplation. The comprehensive account of *eudaimonia*, then, involves the flourishing of all the capacities of the soul that have a share in human excellence.

In addition to these goods of the soul, Aristotle maintains that the flourishing life requires a moderate amount of external goods (1099a31–1099b7). Such external goods can include things outside of one that are not entirely due to one's own choosing or making. These external goods are often the result of fortune or chance. For example, a person must be well born such that they receive the necessary education and nurturing. A person who suffers the misfortunes of poverty or neglect will not be able to achieve *eudaimonia*. We do not blame a person for being born into poverty or neglect, but nor do we think that they will be able to achieve the highest human excellence. A person also needs good friends and family; someone who has all the other goods and yet is friendless or childless we would not regard as living the best kind of life. People who have suffered through the death of many friends or their children are also not enjoying complete human flourishing. Much of our flourishing is thus of our own making, but we also require a moderate amount of prosperity in external goods as well. In addition to making good choices, we also require a measure of good fortune.

Whereas the comprehensive account of *eudaimonia* requires a fulfilment of the several capacities of the soul, Aristotle also develops a conception of *eudaimonia* that focuses exclusively upon fulfilling the highest element in the soul: the rational. This conception of *eudaimonia* is often referred to as the contemplative life or the intellectualist conception of flourishing. Aristotle develops this conception towards the conclusion of the *Nicomachean Ethics*. He rightly observes that the comprehensive account requires the fulfilment of our composite nature: we use reason to satisfy the needs and desires of our bodies and souls. But the life of reason does not, Aristotle argues, involve our composite nature; rather, the life of pure contemplation is 'a thing apart' from our composite nature (1178a22). Recall Aristotle's contention in *On the Soul* that the intellect, or at least some part of it, is not mingled with the body.[5] Aristotle employs that point here in his ethical writings to argue that the life of intellectual contemplation is the highest kind of life achievable by human beings. We can actively contemplate more continuously than we can do any other activity (1177a22). Aristotle holds also that contemplation is the most pleasant activity we can engage in. For a life of contemplation, we need very little external to us (1178a24). We need only enough nourishment to survive; we need only enough wealth to enable us to pursue contemplation. We also do not need friends or family to pursue contemplation. In these respects, the life of contemplation is not dependent upon luck or fortune in the way that the practical life is. For practical success, we need some good fortune. For contemplation, we need very little outside of us. Aristotle also claims that the life of intellectual contemplation is a divine activity (1178b20). God does not act to satisfy needs or desires; rather, god simply contemplates. Thus in aspiring to a life of contemplation, we are satisfying the highest and most divine element in us.

The life of contemplation thus closely resembles the life of the wise person or the sage. This life does not involve political or social activity. Nor does this life require any more external goods than are needed for survival. The contemplative life is devoted to no end other than understanding; practical success is only important insofar as it enables one to pursue what is truly important, i.e. contemplation. We thus see how once again Aristotle values theoretical activity more highly than practical activity. Practical activity is mingled with our bodies, our desires and our social lives; it is concerned with success in these matters. Contemplation is not mingled with our bodies, nor is it dependent on our social or political lives. The highest kind of excellence for human beings, then, is an excellence that is not concerned with practical matters at all; it is instead an excellence of the divine element in us.

We are thus left with the task of reconciling these two different accounts of *eudaimonia*. It seems clear that Aristotle regards the contemplative life as the highest form of human excellence; the life of practical success is secondary. Some have wondered whether Aristotle intended to undermine his account of practical success by presenting the life of contemplation. It is unlikely that this was his intention. It is perhaps more illuminating to view these two accounts of *eudaimonia* through the lens of *On the Soul*. There we saw Aristotle equivocate between two conceptions of human nature. First, he develops a hylemorphic account of human beings as a complex unity of body and soul, matter and form. But he also advances the view that some part of the intellect does not adhere to this hylemorphic model; there is some part of the intellect that has no organ specific to it. Aristotle is deeply compelled by the unique nature of thought and intellect to reconsider his hylemorphic view. In a sense, Aristotle presents two conceptions of human flourishing because he has two conceptions of what a human being is. We are a complex unity of body and soul, but we also partake in the divine activity of thought. Seen in this way, it is entirely appropriate that Aristotle presents two accounts of human flourishing. Aristotle thus presents the highest excellence achievable with respect to our composite nature; this is success or flourishing. In addition, we are presented with the highest excellence achievable with respect to what is divine in our own nature; this is the life of pure contemplation. Most human beings aspire to the life of practical success; for this reason, most of the *Nicomachean Ethics* treats this conception of flourishing. There are also, however, those rare individuals who aspire to a life of contemplation; there may perhaps be only a handful of such individuals in a generation. While such people are rare, Aristotle would value the achievement of their lives more highly than the practical success that most of us seek.

VIRTUES OF CHARACTER

We have now reached the heart of Aristotle's ethics. Given that Aristotle understands ethics as the science of character (*ethos*), it is no surprise that the bulk of the *Nicomachean Ethics* (Books 2–5) deals with matters of character. Aristotle's treatment of matters of character is remarkable for its extraordinary insights into human psychology. Aristotle combines the keen observations of a psychologist, the rigour of a scientist, and the sensitivity of a novelist in producing this treatise on character. While there are certainly puzzles that remain in the details of Aristotle's account, it is also certain that in his general approach and theory Aristotle is basically correct in his study of character. Because of the veracity of this account, Aristotle's study of character is also invaluable as psychological therapy. If your goal is to live well and be successful, you would do well to incorporate Aristotle's lessons for shaping your character.

Aristotle begins by making a few key distinctions to locate and define the virtues of character. Virtues of character are differentiated from the intellectual virtues. Intellectual virtues concern the functioning of the rational element in one's soul; the intellectual virtues of practical wisdom (*praxis*) and contemplation (*theoria*) are the chief virtues of this capacity of the soul. Intellectual excellences are cultivated through teaching and experience (1103a15–19). Virtues of character are the excellences of the irrational part of the soul; virtues of character concern the capacities of perception and desire. While perception and desire are part of the irrational element of the soul, these capacities can have a share in reason; the perceiving and desiring element in the soul can obey or resist reason. Sometimes we desire things that reason tells us we should avoid; in such cases, our reason is either overcome by desire or desire is overcome by reason. When we have desires, we do not simply act to satisfy those desires as animals do; rather, we deliberate and choose whether to satisfy those desires and how best to do so. It is precisely because this irrational element in the soul can have a share in reason that it can become virtuous or vicious. The nutritive capacity of the soul has no share in reason; your digestive tract, for example, does not obey or resist reason's commands. Nor do the processes of growth and maturation share in reason. Because of this, the nutritive capacities of soul have no share in human excellence.

Let us consider how the full range of human character traits can arise out of the perceiving and desiring element in the soul. The capacity of perception begins with the sense of touch; through touch, we perceive certain phenomena as pleasurable and others as painful. We naturally desire that which is pleasurable and we seek to avoid that which is painful. The perceiving and desiring element thus seeks pleasure. Aristotle states that there can be a number of ways in which people's characters can be oriented towards the pursuit of pleasure. For example, some people indulge in excessive pleasures; they may seek the right pleasures, e.g. food and drink, but they pursue these pleasures beyond the point of health. Other people may not desire pleasures enough; such people Aristotle describes as insensitive. There are others who desire the right kinds of pleasure and desire the right amounts of these pleasures; such people exhibit the character trait of temperance or self-control. Recall that our overall goal in life is success or flourishing. Indulgence can harm one's flourishing by ruining one's health or by leading to addiction. Insensitivity undermines our flourishing because we do not enjoy pleasures as much as we should. The virtue of temperance is the state of character that enables one to be successful and flourishing with respect to pleasures and pains in life. Thus with respect to pleasure and pain, there are several states of character that can arise among human beings. These states are due to the way in which the irrational element in the soul, i.e. the perceiving and desiring element, responds to objects of perception. Our irrational element reacts to objects of the perception of touch by desiring these objects too much, too little or the right amount.

The pursuit of pleasure and the avoidance of pain can also affect how we contend with situations that can inspire feelings of fear or confidence. Courage is the virtue of character that concerns our reactions to situations that can produce fear or confidence in us. Once again, then, the character virtues arise through our experience of objects of perception. We perceive events that may be threatening, and we feel fear; if we are pained by fear, we will be unlikely to stand our ground and show courage. There are several states of character that can arise with respect to feelings of fear and confidence. Some people are excessively fearful; they respond to events with more fear than is appropriate. It is also the case that some people are too fearless; such people are not pained enough by the fear that they feel. In between these extremes of cowardice and rashness is the virtue of courage. Courage, then, concerns responding with the right amounts of fear and confidence to the particular events in which we find ourselves.

Another example of a trait of character concerns our temper. We perceive events that can inspire feelings of anger. Some people are too quick to anger; others persist for too long in their anger; some people get too angry; others do not get sufficiently angry when the situation calls for it. The virtue of good temper thus involves feeling the right amount of anger appropriate to the situation in which one finds oneself.

Note that each of these character traits concerns how we perceive and respond to circumstances. These responses are not rational; whether we get angry, fearful or indulgent is not due to reason; rather, these character traits concern the desires and emotions that human beings experience. Aristotle rightly views these responses as part of the irrational element in the soul. Desires and emotions can make your life more pleasant or more difficult. The goal for Aristotle is to train your desires and emotions such that you respond to situations in ways that lead to success. This involves training your desires and emotions to obey reason. If you are the kind of person, for example, who always gets angry in various situations and you cannot control your anger using reason, the success of your life is likely to be harmed by your excessive anger. You are either going to be tormented by your uncontrollable anger, or you may even provoke others into harming you because of your excessive anger. The same patterns can be observed with excessive fear or indulgence. People who cannot control their desire for wine, for example, are not likely to lead a successful and flourishing life. They are far more likely to ruin their lives through disease. Aristotle's study of character is remarkable because it acknowledges the fundamental importance of desire and emotion in leading a successful and happy life. Someone tormented by desire and emotion is not likely to be successful or happy. Becoming good, then, is not just a matter of developing reason; becoming good crucially involves developing the traits of character that are likely to lead to success and happiness.

While the virtues of reason arise through teaching, the virtues of character arise through habit (1103a15–20). Aristotle notes the etymological connection between the words for *character* and *habit*; in Greek, these words are nearly identical.[6] From this etymological point Aristotle draws the illuminating conclusion that our character traits are due to habit. This is surely a correct psychological observation about human beings: as the saying goes, we are creatures of habit. People who are indulgent are habitually indulgent; they consistently desire more pleasure than is appropriate. With eating and drinking, for example, some people get into habits of eating too much or drinking too much; by consistently eating or drinking too much, you become the kind of person who eats or drinks too much. The kind of person we become, then, is due to the kinds of habits that we form. Thus Aristotle's conclusion: 'It makes no small difference, then, whether we form habits of one kind or another from our very youth; it makes a very great difference, or rather *all* the difference' (1103b24–25). The kinds of habits we develop shape the kind of person we become. Further, these habits form from a very young age; children who are raised with indulgent habits are likely to become indulgent people. Their chances of success are greatly harmed by the development of poor habits.

Aristotle notes that the virtues of character do not arise in us by nature. This is a key point regarding our states of character, though this point is easily misunderstood. Consider Aristotle's statement of this thesis:

[N]one of the moral excellences arise in us by nature; for nothing that exists by nature can form a habit contrary to its nature. For instance the stone which by nature moves downwards cannot be habituated to move upwards, not even if one tries to train it by throwing it up ten thousand times; nor can fire be habituated to move downwards, nor can anything else that by nature behaves in one way be trained to behave in another. Neither by nature, then, nor contrary to nature do excellences arise in us; rather we are adapted by nature to receive them, and are made perfect by habit. (1103a19–25)

The example of the stone is helpful; a stone by nature behaves such that when left unimpeded it moves downwards. A stone cannot be conditioned or habituated to behave in any other way. All things that are due to nature, then, happen always or for the most part in the same way. States of character, however, are not like this. With respect to pleasure we saw how some people become temperate, others indulgent and still others insensitive. There is no one way that all human beings become with respect to pleasure. The variety of different states of character thus suggests to Aristotle that humans are not naturally disposed to become temperate or courageous. We can develop any of a number of states of character, and we do this through the habits we develop. The last line of the above passage is also important: 'we are adapted by nature to receive them, and are made perfect by habit' (1103a25). By nature, then, we develop habits that lead to a state of character; but there is no one way in which all of us develop. We do not all tend to become virtuous, for example; nor do we all tend to become vicious. But we all do become some kind of person; it is inevitable and necessary that we develop, through habit, certain states of character. This is part of the maturation of a human being. For example, it is not possible for a human being to remain neutral with respect to pleasure; we are the kind of creature that will develop *some* trait of character with respect to pleasure. *Which* trait of character we develop is due to the habits that we form. The same is true with anger and fear. It is inevitable that we develop some kind of temper; we cannot say of any human being that he has no temper. As human beings, we will develop a pattern or habit for dealing with particular desires or emotions; the habits we form shape the person we become. Aristotle's great insight here is that to some extent the habits we form are up to us; thus the character we shape for ourselves is up to us. It is true that parents and teachers inculcate certain habits in the young, but we still have a great deal of control over our character. We control our actions; our actions give rise to our habits; our habits shape our character; our character is who we are.

Aristotle's thesis that virtues of character do not arise by nature is sometimes interpreted as the claim that none of us has any natural dispositions of character. This is not, however, how Aristotle's thesis should be interpreted. Aristotle's claim is not that individual human beings have no natural dispositions, but rather his claim is that human beings do not all have the same natural dispositions of character. Human beings often exhibit tendencies or dispositions in their characters from a very young age. Aristotle's point is that we do not all exhibit the same tendencies. If a good temper arose by nature, all of us would exhibit the same disposition towards a good temper. Consider again the example of the stone in the above passage: *all* stones tend to move downwards if left unimpeded. With human character traits, the situation is different. We all have natural dispositions, but we do not all have the *same* dispositions. Some of us are disposed to being excessively fearful; others are disposed to fearlessness; still others are disposed to courage. In order to become good, we must come to understand our own natural dispositions. Those of us who are pained by fear, for example, may have to work harder to cultivate the virtue of courage. In this respect as in many others, Aristotle's approach is true. His theory would surely be in error if he denied that human beings have any natural dispositions of character. Rather, his theory acknowledges that we do have such natural dispositions, but that these dispositions are extremely varied.

Human beings are thus not naturally disposed to virtue or vice; rather, we are able to become virtuous or vicious, and this occurs through our actions and our habits. Our character is thus shaped by our actions and habits. In drawing this conclusion, Aristotle likens the virtues of character to the arts:

> [E]xcellences we get by first exercising them, as also happiness in the case of the arts as well. For the things we have to learn before we can do, we learn by doing, e.g. men become builders by building and lyre-players by playing the lyre; so too we become just by doing just acts, temperate by doing temperate acts, brave by doing brave acts. (1103a30–1103b1)

This comparison is continued in another passage:

> Again, it is from the same causes and by the same means that every excellence is both produced and destroyed, and similarly every art; for it is from playing the lyre that both good and bad lyre-players are produced. And the corresponding statement is true of builders and of all the rest; men will be good or bad builders as a result of building well or badly. For if this were not so, there would have been no need of a teacher, but all men would have been born good or bad at their craft. This, then, is the case with the excellences also; by doing the acts that we do in our transactions with other men we become just or unjust, and by doing the acts that we do in the presence of danger, and being habituated to feel fear or confidence, we become brave or cowardly. The same is true of appetites and feelings of anger; some men become temperate and good-tempered, others self-indulgent and irascible, by behaving in one way or the other in the appropriate circumstances. Thus, in a word, states arise out of like activities. (1103b6–20)

The comparison with the arts helps to illuminate Aristotle's view on how the virtues of character are formed. Students of Socrates may note at this point that in likening virtues to the arts or crafts (*technai*), Aristotle is adopting a familiar Greek view about the virtues. In the early dialogues, Socrates famously argued that virtue is a craft; for Socrates, being virtuous involves coming to master a body of knowledge.[7] Though Aristotle also uses the comparison with the arts to explain the virtues, it must be noted that for Aristotle and Socrates the comparison is importantly different. For Socrates, the virtues are like the arts because the virtues are a body of knowledge that one must master; Socrates' conception of the virtues is strictly intellectual. For Aristotle, however, the virtues are like the arts because both are areas where we learn by doing. The virtues of character are not bodies of knowledge; as Aristotle has clearly shown, the virtues of character concern our desires and emotions in response to situations. Aristotle draws this contrast between his view and Socrates': 'Socrates, then, thought the excellences were forms of reason (for he thought they were, all of them, forms of knowledge), while we think they *involve* reason' (1144b28–29).[8] The virtues, then, involve reason, but they are not simply forms of reason or knowledge. In the final section of this chapter, we shall investigate Aristotle's notion of practical wisdom, which is the form of reason involved in the virtues. Thus while both Aristotle and Socrates liken the virtues to the arts, they do so for different reasons. Socrates emphasizes the intellectual aspect of the arts and virtues, while Aristotle emphasizes that the arts and virtues are activities.

In the above passages Aristotle demonstrates that the states of character arise out of like activities. It is thus clear that states of character are not produced by a single act; rather, it is through consistent and repeated actions that we produce our states of character. As human beings, we find ourselves throughout our lives in various situations. Some situations require us to transact with other human beings. How we perform in such transactions determines the state of character we produce; by behaving justly in these situations, we become just. We also find ourselves in situations where we feel desires for pleasure; in acting indulgently in such situations, we become indulgent; in acting temperately in such situations, we become temperate. It is thus clear why Aristotle emphasizes the importance of forming the right habits. With the arts, someone who has built poorly in many instances will likely become a poor builder; once these poor building habits are ingrained in the person, it is very difficult to change those habits in order to become a good builder. The builder has already established a pattern for acting and building. The same analysis obtains with the states of character. A person who habitually behaves indulgently will become an indulgent person; in order to become a temperate person, this would require the development of new habits. One has to perform temperate actions to become temperate. For an indulgent person, this is very difficult because he or she would have to overcome years of habit. It is thus the duty of the state and the parents to raise young people in the right habits; if we raise young people in the wrong habits, we make it nearly impossible for them to become virtuous.

Ultimately, we settle upon courses of action because of pleasures and pains. This is obvious with respect to temperance, but it is also the case with respect to the other virtues of character. For example, with respect to the virtue of courage, whether we stand our ground and fight or flee is due to feelings of pleasure and pain. If fearsome and terrible things pain us, then we will be less likely to stand our ground. The person who feels pleasure at facing such threats is more likely to be courageous. Consider Aristotle's statement:

For moral excellence is concerned with pleasures and pains; it is on account of pleasure that we do bad things, and on account of pain that we abstain from noble ones. Hence we ought to have been brought up in a particular way from our very youth, as Plato says, so as both to delight in and to be pained by the things that we ought; for this is the right education. (1104b9–13)

We have seen the importance of habit in shaping our character; it is now clear that the way in which we develop the habits that lead to virtue is through being properly trained with respect to pleasures and pains. This reinforces Aristotle's point that becoming virtuous involves a total training of one's character. We need to be pleased by virtuous acts and pained by vicious ones. Someone who is raised, for example, to be pleased by the indulgent pursuit of pleasure will see no reason why he should become temperate. To this person, temperance is painful. To the temperate person, however, it is pleasurable to abstain from bodily pleasures and it is painful to yield to bodily pleasures. Aristotle's account of the virtues thus acknowledges the central role that pleasure and pain have in guiding human action. What we do, we do on account of pleasures and pains; it is thus vital that we train our desires so that we are properly affected.

Let us characterize more precisely Aristotle's notion of being properly affected by pleasures and pains. The key idea guiding Aristotle's account is that some pleasures are *by nature* pleasant: 'the lovers of what is noble find pleasant the things that are by nature pleasant' (1099a13). Being properly affected, then, involves finding pleasant the things that are by nature pleasant. What make something pleasant by nature? The simple fact that such a thing is good for us, i.e. that it contributes to our human flourishing. Thus the virtuous person finds pleasant the things that contribute to her success and flourishing, and she finds painful those things that harm her flourishing. People who are not properly affected by pleasures and pains find pleasure in things that are not by nature pleasant. For example, eating properly and exercising are by nature pleasant; these things contribute to human flourishing. But some people do not find proper eating and exercise habits pleasant; such people do not find pleasure in what is by nature pleasant. Instead they find pleasure in excessive eating and inactivity; while they may find these things pleasant, such pleasures harm their human flourishing because they compromise a person's health. When we educate our youth incorrectly, then, we raise them to find pleasant things that are not by nature pleasant; further, we raise them to be pained by things that are by nature pleasant. Thus the task of being properly affected is to be pleased by things that are by nature pleasant and to be pained by things that are by nature painful.

Aristotle's account thus leads to an interesting conclusion: the virtuous life and virtuous actions are pleasant to the virtuous person. The temperate person, for example, finds it easy to act temperately; she is already inculcated in these habits and thus she finds pleasant moderation with respect to pleasure. As Aristotle says, for the virtuous person pleasure completes the activity (1174b24). Thus virtuous actions flow naturally and easily from the virtuous person's character; virtuous actions are also accompanied by a feeling of pleasure at performing a virtuous action. Aristotle's account is noteworthy for its contrast with other prominent approaches to ethics. Many ethical theories hold that being virtuous can be difficult or painful; being virtuous may involve making a sacrifice. For Aristotle, however, the good life is pleasant and easy for the good person. The good life is not characterized by struggle, torment or temptation. Instead, the good life for Aristotle is characterized by an agreement between our desires and what is naturally desirable; acting virtuously is thus its own pleasure. This is not, however, to suggest that no one struggles with temptation on Aristotle's account. The vast majority of people do experience such a struggle because they desire the wrong things. The goal of Aristotle's ethics is to become the kind of person who does not struggle. For those who are not virtuous, it is a painful struggle to try to be virtuous; but for those who are virtuous, it is pleasant and easy to be virtuous. Aristotle's account shows that there is nothing noble or honourable in struggling to be virtuous in the face of pain; it is much better to be virtuous without any struggle at all.

Sometimes we desire things that are by nature bad for us. In many cases, however, the problem lies not in what we desire but in how much of it we desire. Both the virtuous and vicious persons can desire the same things, but the virtuous person will desire the right amount of these things, while the vicious person will desire either too much or too little of these things. This observation leads Aristotle to his famous doctrine of the mean; this doctrine holds that virtue is a mean between two extremes. Consider Aristotle's first formulation of the doctrine:

First, then, let us consider this, that it is the nature of such things [virtues of character] to be destroyed by defect and excess, as we see in the case of strength and of health (for to gain light on things imperceptible we must use the evidence of sensible things); both excessive and defective exercise destroy the strength, and similarly drink or food which is above or below a certain amount destroys the health, while that which is proportionate both produces and increases and preserves it. So too is it, then, in the case of temperance and courage and the other excellences. For the man who flies from and fears everything and does not stand his ground against anything becomes a coward, and the man who fears nothing at all but goes to meet every danger becomes rash, and similarly the man who indulges in every pleasure and abstains from none becomes self-indulgent, while the man who shuns every pleasure, as boors do, becomes in a way insensible; temperance and courage, then, are destroyed by excess and defect, and preserved by the mean. (1104a11–26)

Aristotle begins with a comparison between the health of the body and the virtues of character. We know that the health of the body and the virtues of character are both states that are produced by actions. We want to know, then, not only what are the states at which to aim, but also how to preserve those states once we have achieved them.

Aristotle follows a familiar pattern to investigate this issue: he begins with an example that is clearer to us to illuminate the subject that is more obscure. Most people have a clearer idea of bodily health than they do of the virtues of character; thus he will illuminate the latter by means of the former. Bodily health is preserved by the mean and is destroyed by excess and deficiency. It is not just exercise that preserves the health of the body, but rather the right amount and kind of exercise. How do we determine what is the right amount and kind of exercise? We do so by observing the kind of exercise that the strong and healthy person performs. That is the standard at which we should aim. Aristotle also notes that there is a reinforcement loop with respect to the physical health of the body. Strength 'is produced by taking much food and undergoing much exertion, and it is the strong man that will be most able to do these things' (1103a31). Once we establish the health of our bodies, then, we are better able to do the things that will preserve the health of our body. For the strong person, doing the things that make one strong is pleasant and easy. The person who is weak and infirm will find the eating and exercise habits of a healthy person both painful and difficult.

A similar analysis obtains for the virtues of character. Our character traits are states that arise from like activities (1103b20). The virtues of character are means between two extreme states of character. Consider the virtue of courage. Some may think that a person is either courageous or cowardly; there are two options, one of which is a virtue, the other of which is a vice. But Aristotle rejects this analysis. It is not the case that virtue is one extreme and vice is the other; rather, every virtue is a mean between two vices that form the extremes. One can fall short of courage by being excessively fearful; this is the vice of cowardice. One can also fall short of courage by being excessively fearless; this is the vice of rashness. A courageous person does not exhibit complete confidence and lack of fear; rather, the courageous person exhibits the confidence and fear that are appropriate to the situation. This is the mean between cowardice and rashness. Just as with physical health, there is a reinforcement loop with respect to the virtues:

> [B]y abstaining from pleasures we become temperate, and it is when we have become so that we are most able to abstain from them; and similarly too in the case of courage; for by being habituated to despise things that are terrible and to stand our ground against them we become brave, and it is when we have become so that we shall be most able to stand our ground against them. (1104a33–1104b2)

Once we achieve the virtue of character, it is easy and pleasant to perform acts that preserve this state. Just as the strong person is the standard of physical health, so the virtuous person is the standard for traits of character. How do we know what is the right amount of fear and confidence to feel in a given situation? We know by observing the courageous person; the amount of fear and confidence he exhibits is the mean. Thus the virtuous person sets the standard for virtuous action.

To understand the doctrine of the mean, it is helpful to keep in mind Aristotle's principle of excess and defect in *Physics*.[9] Aristotle introduces the notion of excess and defect as a way to explain all

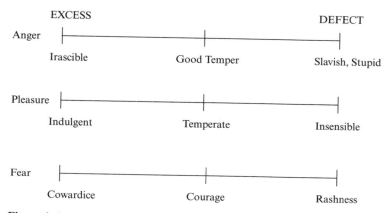

SUCCESS (*EUDAIMONIA*)

Figure 4. A representation of the mean for selected virtues.

possible changes among natural substances. We noted that Aristotle conceives of change as the movement from one extreme end of a continuum to another. While excess and defect are raised in Aristotle's ethics for a different reason, the conception of excess and defect as forming a continuum is applicable to the doctrine of the mean. Figure 4 provides a few diagrams to represent virtues and the mean.

In using the concepts of excess and deficiency as applied to human actions and responses, Aristotle emphasizes that our actions and responses are best seen as forming a continuum of possible actions and responses. There is a tremendous range of possible actions for human beings. When we choose to act, we choose not between two options; instead, we choose among many possible actions. This is one reason why excellence is rare and difficult to achieve; we must assess each situation and react with the appropriate action; this action will be a mean between the extremes of excess and defect.

It is also helpful to remember Aristotle's image of the archer aiming for a target. Like the archer, when we act we aim at the target; we have a goal for our actions. While it is true that either we hit the target or we miss it, there are many ways to miss the target. There is only one way to be virtuous, but there are many ways to miss the mark and fall short of virtue. Consider the example of anger. People can be bad-tempered in many ways. Some people are too quick to anger; some get angry too often; some feel too much anger; others stay angry for too long. There are numerous ways in which we can go wrong with respect to our temper, but there is only one way to get it right. Here is Aristotle's statement of the challenge we face:

> Hence also it is no easy task to be good. For in everything it is no easy task to find the middle, e.g. to find the middle of a circle is not for everyone but for him who knows; so, too, anyone can get angry – that is easy – or give or spend money; but to do this to the right person, to the right extent, at the right time, with the right aim, and in the right way, *that* is not for everyone, nor is it easy; that is why goodness is both rare and laudable and noble. (1109a24–29)

Note the numerous qualifications Aristotle makes regarding right action: anger cannot be misdirected, it cannot be excessive or deficient, it must have a proper aim and it must be done in the right way. This is not easy, but the virtuous person succeeds at precisely this. Note also that on Aristotle's account, we are not in principle wrong to feel anger; anger is not inherently wrong, nor is fear or the desire for pleasure. There are inappropriate ways to express one's anger, but there are appropriate and excellent ways to express these feelings and to act based on these feelings. We can consider a more simplistic model of human action: some may argue that certain emotions like anger are always wrong and should be avoided; likewise desire is always wrong or sinful and should be avoided. Aristotle rejects the model that human emotions or desires are inherently wrong. Instead, he develops a more subtle and nuanced approach that leaves it up to the virtuous person to determine their target and to take action to hit the target.

The images of the continuum and the archer's target are thus useful ways to visualize Aristotle's doctrine of the mean. He further clarifies this doctrine by drawing an important distinction to help us determine the mean. Aristotle argues that in determining the mean, we must seek the mean *relative to us* and not the mean *in the object*. Here is his statement of the distinction:

> By the intermediate in the object I mean that which is equidistant from each of the extremes, which is one and the same for all men; by the intermediate relatively to us that which is neither too much nor too little – and this is not one, nor the same for all. For

instance, if ten is many and two is few, six is intermediate, taken in terms of the object; for it exceeds and is exceeded by an equal amount; this is intermediate according to arithmetical proportion. But the intermediate relatively to us is not to be taken so; if ten pounds are too much for a particular person to eat and two too little, it does not follow that the trainer will order six pounds; for this is also perhaps too much for the person who is to take it, or too little – too little for Milo, too much for the beginner in athletic exercises. The same is true of running and wrestling. Thus a master of any art avoids excess and defect, but seeks the intermediate and chooses this – the intermediate not in the object but relatively to us. (1106a29–1106b5)

Aristotle once again illustrates an important distinction using a comparison with physical health. In physical health, we must consider actions that are intermediate relative to us. Our own capacities for action and our own physical states must thus be considered in every action; it is with respect to these that we determine the mean. This is not the same for all human beings; each of us is different, and so the mean relative to each of us will be different. By considering the mean relative to the object, we might conclude that the mean is the same for all human beings; but Aristotle argues that this is not the case with physical health or the virtues of character. The recipe for physical health is not the same for every individual; rather, the doctor or trainer must consider what is appropriate in each case. Again, we see Aristotle reject universal rules for physical health and for ethics; our situations and dispositions are too varied for one rule to apply to all of us. Instead, we must consider ourselves as individuals, and seek the mean relative to us.

Let us further clarify how determining the mean relative to us obtains in the case of virtues of character. As we noted above, Aristotle states that many of us have certain natural dispositions with respect to states of character. We do not, however, all have the same dispositions of character. This means that when we determine the mean relative to us, we must consider our own affective capacities and the tendencies of our own natural dispositions. Consider:

But we must consider the things toward which we ourselves also are easily carried away; for some of us tend to one thing, some to another; and this will be recognizable from the pleasure and pain we feel. We must drag ourselves away to the contrary extreme; for we shall get into the intermediate state by drawing well away from error, as people do in straightening sticks that are bent. (1109b2–6)

Aristotle here shows how our own natural dispositions can drag us away from the mean towards one of the extremes. In order to determine the mean relative to us, we must consider the ways in which we are dragged to one extreme or the other. Just as bent sticks are straightened, so also our *bent* characters are straightened by becoming aware of our own dispositions. If we tend towards excessive fear, we must drag ourselves away from that extreme and towards the mean. When we are pulled towards one extreme or the other, we destroy the virtues; the virtues are preserved by the mean. We must thus determine the actions that preserve the mean, and this will be determined differently for each of us.

It is also the case that circumstances can affect a shift in the mean. The mean is thus not the same in every situation in which we find ourselves. For example, what is rash in one context may be appropriate in another. Extreme anger may be appropriate if someone is threatening your child, but it is entirely inappropriate as a response to an unintentional slight. The mean in each of these circumstances is different, hence the conclusion that the circumstances in which we find ourselves can cause a shift in the mean. This is yet another reason why it is difficult to be good: you have to determine the mean for you in each given situation. The mean is thus both relative to each person and relative to each situation.

With this understanding of the virtues and the doctrine of the mean established, Aristotle provides his most precise account of virtue: 'Excellence, then, is a state concerned with choice, lying in a mean relative to us, this being determined by reason and in the way in which the man of practical wisdom would determine it' (1106b35–1107a2). Each aspect of this account is crucial. Aristotle has established that the excellences are states of character; these states are formed by habitual action. These states also have a degree of fixity; they are stable and thus not liable to fluctuation. These states of character are also voluntarily chosen. While we all have certain natural dispositions, these do not determine our character. There exists a range of voluntary choices regarding our actions, and we are responsible for the actions we choose. Since the actions we choose shape our character, we are thus responsible for the character we have. This is why, Aristotle says, we are praised or blamed for being virtuous or vicious; we recognize that becoming virtuous or vicious depends to a great extent on voluntary choices regarding our actions. We are not praised or blamed for things that happen involuntarily; this is why no one is commended for her processes of digestion or the growth of her body, for example. We have also investigated the sense in which the virtues are preserved by the mean relative to us. We determine the mean relative to us using practical wisdom. Our guide in this process is the person of practical wisdom; it is he or she who sets the standard for virtue and virtuous action. It remains for us to treat Aristotle's notion of practical wisdom and how it contributes to a successful and flourishing life.

VIRTUES OF INTELLECT

Up to this point we have discussed the virtues of character, which are a part of the irrational element in the soul. These virtues of character are not wholly irrational, however; they have a share in reason insofar as the irrational yields to or resists the dictates of reason. In addition, the mean is determined by reason. The virtues of character thus concern our feelings and desires in a given situation, while the element of reason determines what is the best course of action to bring about the desired end. This feature of reason is not the whole of reason, but is rather a specific part of the rational element in the soul. It is clear, then, that for Aristotle the virtues involve reason; reason alone is not sufficient for virtue, but neither can one become virtuous without reason. Excellence thus requires a combination of the excellences of character and the excellences of intellect. Book 6 of the *Nicomachean Ethics* concerns this intellectual excellence that is necessary for achieving success and flourishing. We shall thus investigate the nature and role of intellectual excellence in the good life.

When Aristotle first differentiated the character virtues from the intellectual virtues, he noted that the former arise through habit while the latter arise through teaching, experience and time (1103a14–19). Our emotions and desires are thus subject to habituation; how we are affected is the result of repeated actions that we perform. The case of intellect is different, for we cannot be habituated to make good decisions. Reason is not an instrument of habit; rather, reason seeks understanding and justification. To use this rational element properly, we must be instructed in how to use reason. This instruction can take several forms. Teachers can instruct us in how to use reason. Experience and time are also teachers; by having experiences and developing memories about our past decisions and actions, we learn from these events and apply what we have learned to future decisions and actions. This contrast between the virtues of character and the virtues of intellect is important for understanding the separate roles of these virtues in the good life. Habituation produces the virtues of character; learning produces the virtues of intellect. Aristotle's theory of a human being rightly draws a distinction between two different kinds of excellence and the different means that produce those excellences.

With intellectual virtue distinguished from character virtue, Aristotle next seeks to determine what part of the intellect is concerned with living well. We know that ethics concerns action; on this basis it is classified as a practical science. Living well does not involve productive or theoretical reason; living well does not require the production of an artefact, nor is living well brought about through theoretical understanding. The aspect of reason of interest to ethics, then, is that part of reason concerned with action. Aristotle refers to this aspect of reason as the deliberative faculty because it contemplates that which could be otherwise. This is distinct from the scientific faculty of reason, which contemplates that which cannot be otherwise (1139a5–17). We have seen how ethics is a science that lacks fixity; ethics exhibits much variety and fluctuation. For this reason, the precision and exactness of ethics does not match that of the theoretical sciences. The theoretical sciences do not exhibit variety and fluctuation; the principles of the theoretical sciences are true and immutable. The reason that contemplates theoretical science is thus not deliberative, for one cannot deliberate about that which cannot be otherwise.

Now that we understand which part of reason is concerned with acting well, we need to inquire as to two questions: what does this deliberative faculty contemplate and what is its excellence? Aristotle first demonstrates the connection between the deliberative faculty and action: 'The origin of action – its efficient, not its final cause – is choice, and that of choice is desire and reasoning with a view to an end' (1139a31–32). For us to act, we must choose. For us to choose, we must have both desire and reasoning. We act because we desire something, and we use reason to determine the means to satisfy our desire, i.e. how to achieve our end. We know that our desires are concerned with pleasures and pains; further, our pleasures and pains arise from things that are by nature good for us or by nature bad for us. Thus this deliberative faculty contemplates how to achieve the ends set by our desires for what is good or bad for us. Our desires must be trained and habituated to enjoy the right things and avoid the wrong things. The deliberative faculty does not determine what ends we seek; instead, it contemplates the means that we can pursue to achieve the ends set by our desires. Thus we arrive at Aristotle's definition of this deliberative faculty: 'it is a true and reasoned state of capacity to act with regard to the things that are good or bad for man' (1140b4–5). It remains to be seen what is the excellence of this deliberative faculty.

In order to determine the excellence of this deliberative faculty, Aristotle argues that we must look to those whom we credit with using this faculty well. The people who exhibit the excellence of this faculty are our best guide for discovering the nature of its excellence. In general, when reasoning is true, we call this state *wisdom*. The wisdom we are concerned with here is not theoretical wisdom or productive wisdom; rather, we are concerned with *practical* wisdom, i.e. true and successful deliberations about how to act to achieve a desired end. Here is Aristotle's first statement concerning practical wisdom, which is the excellence of the deliberative faculty:

> Now it is thought to be a mark of a man of practical wisdom to be able to deliberate well about what is good and expedient for himself, not in some particular respect, e.g. about what sorts of things conduce to health or to strength, but about what sorts of things conduce to the good life in general. (1140a25–28)

In this passage we see the standard against which the deliberative faculty is judged: we deliberate well insofar as we are successful in achieving the desired ends, and we deliberate poorly insofar as we fail to achieve our desired ends. There is no other standard for practical wisdom than success in action; to have practical wisdom, one must succeed with reference to one's end. The virtue of practical wisdom is thus a successful ability to deliberate about the best means to achieve a desired end. This excellence is not knowledge because it concerns that which can be otherwise. Nor is this excellence an art because its goal is action and not production. Thus Aristotle concludes that the virtue of practical wisdom is 'correctness of thinking' (1142b13).

Practical wisdom is thus a correctness of thinking with respect to what is good or bad for human beings. Aristotle seeks to give a more precise account of the functioning of practical wisdom. He approaches this topic by considering how practical wisdom contemplates universals and particulars. Consider:

> The man who is without qualification good at deliberating is the man who is capable of aiming in accordance with calculation at the best for man of things attainable by action. Nor is practical wisdom concerned with universals only – it must also recognize the particulars; for it is practical and practice is concerned with particulars. This is why some who do not know, and especially those who have experience, are more practical than others who know; for if a man knew that light meats are digestible and wholesome, but did not know which sorts of meat are light, he would not produce health, but the man who knows that chicken is wholesome is more likely to produce health. (1141b12–20)

Practical wisdom thus involves knowledge of universals, but it also requires the ability to recognize particulars as instantiations of these universals. For example, a person who knows the universal rule that light meats are digestible and wholesome but is not able to recognize particular meats as being light does not evidence practical wisdom. We must both know the universal and be able to recognize the universal in the particular.

It is easy to see why Aristotle emphasizes particulars in his account of practical wisdom. We do not act *in general* or *universally*; instead, we act in particular situations. In order to be successful in these situations, we must be able to recognize these particular situations for what they are. Aristotle continues, 'practical wisdom is concerned with the ultimate particular, which is the object not of knowledge but of perception' (1142a26–27). Universals are objects of knowledge, while particulars are objects of perception. When we deliberate, then, we must perceive the relevant details of each particular situation, and we must determine how best to achieve our desired end with reference to this particular situation. This perception is not simply perception of colour or other qualities; rather, it is perception of the various features and characteristics of an event or situation.

It may be helpful to consider this point in the light of Aristotle's comparison of ethics with the arts of navigation and medicine (1104a1–9). Like navigation and medicine, ethics is a field that lacks clear and stable rules or precepts. In these sciences, Aristotle says, 'the agents themselves must in each case consider what is appropriate to the occasion' (1104a8–9). A doctor, for example, does not heal humanity in general; rather, a doctor tries to heal a particular human being. A doctor has general training regarding health, but he must be able to recognize the signs of health or illness in each particular human being. A particular human being is an object of perception, and so medicine, like ethics, is concerned with objects of perception. A similar analysis holds for navigation. In all these cases, the best that we can do is develop an understanding of the central concepts of the science, whether it be health as in medicine or success as in ethics. From this understanding of the goal of the science, it is up to the individual to apply that understanding in particular situations.

Aristotle notes several consequences of the fact that practical wisdom is concerned with universals and particulars, objects of knowledge and objects of perception. First, Aristotle observes that exactness and perfection are far more difficult to achieve with objects of perception. This means that it is very difficult to determine the mean exactly using practical wisdom. Here is Aristotle's statement of the issue:

> The man, however, who deviates little from goodness is not blamed, whether he does so in the direction of the more or of the less, but only the man who deviates more widely; for *he* does not fail to be noticed. But up to what point and to what extent a man must deviate before he becomes blameworthy it is not easy to determine by reasoning, any more than anything else that is perceived by the senses; such things depend on particular facts, and the decision rests with perception. (1109b17–23)

We employ practical wisdom to determine the mean, but because this is an object of perception, it is difficult to determine the mean exactly. Thus we often deviate a little from the mean, but we should not be blamed for such deviation. We cannot determine the mean exactly every time, because that degree of precision is not possible in the science of ethics. Thus while we use practical wisdom to determine the mean, we should not be blamed if we deviate from the mean a little. Because ethics is an inexact science, perfection cannot be expected of human actions.

Aristotle also concludes that we must have experience of many particulars before we can be said to have practical wisdom. Practical wisdom is success at acting with respect to particulars, and the only way to develop this expertise is to have and learn from numerous experiences. As further evidence for this view, Aristotle notes that we do not find young people who have practical wisdom. Young people can be prodigies of mathematics or geometry, but there is no such thing as a prodigy of practical wisdom. This is because practical wisdom is acquired only through experience. Consider:

> What has been said is confirmed by the fact that while young men become geometricians and mathematicians and wise in matters like these, it is thought that a young man of practical wisdom cannot be found. The cause is that such wisdom is concerned not only with universals but with particulars, which become familiar from experience, but a young man has no experience, for it is length of time that gives experience. (1142a11–15)

Thus while young people can become prodigies of the theoretical sciences, there are no prodigies of the fields that require experience. The case is similar with medicine and navigation. A doctor with no experience at healing particular individuals is not yet an excellent doctor; he may have knowledge of health, but he has yet to develop experience with the particulars that are the domain of his practice. Likewise, an inexperienced ship's captain is not yet an excellent navigator; one must have experience with varied conditions and situations in order to have the experience that makes one excellent in the art of navigation. Practical wisdom, then, is not a young person's virtue; it is a virtue that arises though much experience with particular situations.

We now have all of the major pieces of Aristotle's ethics in place; we have surveyed the chief and final good as well as the means by which we can achieve that good, i.e. virtues of character and intellect. Early in the *Nicomachean Ethics*, Aristotle asks if it is sufficient to simply perform the same actions that the virtuous person performs. With these elements of his ethical philosophy now understood, we can better appreciate Aristotle's response to this key question. After all, if ethics is all about action, can we not just imitate the virtuous person's actions? Aristotle argues that it is not simply doing the same thing that the virtuous person does, but it is the way the act is done that is critical. His focus is primarily upon one's character; actions are important only insofar as they help to produce a virtuous character. Consider:

> The agent also must be in a certain condition when he does them [virtuous actions]; in the first place he must have knowledge, secondly he must choose acts, and choose them for their own sakes, and thirdly his action must proceed from a firm and unchangeable character . . . Actions, then, are called just and temperate when they are such as the just or the temperate man would do; but it is not the man who does these that is just and temperate, but the man who also does them *as* just and temperate men do them. (1105a30–1105b1, 1105b5–7)

Aristotle lays out three criteria for evaluating the actions of a person. It is clearly not sufficient to simply imitate the virtuous person. One must act with knowledge. Our discussion of practical wisdom helps to illuminate this criterion: we have knowledge when we know the universal and are able to recognize the universal in the particular objects of perception. We cannot be virtuous by accident; one can perform a virtuous act by accident, but this does not make one a virtuous person. Aristotle states that we must also choose the acts for their own sakes. Two points are important in this criterion. First, virtuous acts must be freely chosen; one is not virtuous if one does a virtuous act under compulsion. Second, virtuous acts must be chosen for their own sakes. If one performs a virtuous act for the sake of some other end or goal, then one is not being virtuous. One must freely choose the virtuous act, and one must choose the virtuous act because it is virtuous and for no other reason.

The final criterion developed in the above passage concerns the 'firm and unchangeable character' from which our actions must proceed. It often happens that human beings perform actions that are *out of character*; someone who is indulgent, for example, may on occasion abstain from pleasure. To be virtuous, however, it must be the case that your actions are entirely in accordance with your firm and unchangeable character. This means that your character is already established through like activities; you have formed the right habits and performed numerous virtuous actions. The firmness of one's character also refers to the fact that your desires are stable and not liable to fluctuation. Further, to be virtuous one must desire things that are by nature pleasant. A virtuous person with a firm and unchangeable character is thus someone who has an established pattern of desire and choice; she consistently desires things that are by nature good for her, and she freely chooses such things for their own sake using her practical wisdom. In such a person, desire and practical wisdom are in harmony; a virtuous person does not have discord in her soul. Rather, her character desires the right ends, and practical wisdom appropriately judges the means to secure those ends. This is what the life of the virtuous person is like. Every aspect of the person's soul is properly focused on achieving success. Our target, then, cannot simply be the actions of the virtuous person; instead, our target must be the character of the virtuous person. We must not aim only to do the same acts as the virtuous person, but to be the kind of person the virtuous person is.

We have now surveyed the main tenets of Aristotle's extraordinary ethical theory. Our focus has been on the features of the practical science of ethics. We have also examined the good at which all human beings aim, and the virtues of intellect and character that are essential to achieving this chief and final good. We have seen how in its focus and approach Aristotle's virtue ethics is vastly different from conventional moral theories. While Aristotle offers a robust and fertile ethical theory, his theory does not deal with many issues that conventional moral philosophers find central to ethics. Indeed, many utilitarian and deontological theorists dispute whether virtue ethics can be properly considered moral philosophy at all. In response to their objections, Aristotle can return to his points about the impossibility of capturing moral rightness in a set of rules. If there are no clear rules by which we can discern what is right, then the project of conventional moral theory will struggle to meet the demands it faces. There is much at stake in this debate between conventional moral theory and virtue ethics. Even those conventional ethical theories that make room for an account of the virtues do so only in a secondary and supplementary way. For Aristotle, the virtues are the entirety of ethics; there is nothing else you need to live well. Concepts like moral rightness and duty actually hinder our ability to live well, according to Aristotle. While we cannot hope to settle this profound conflict in moral theory, we have made considerable progress in detailing the nature of the conflict and explaining the competing intuitions that lead to these very different approaches to ethical theory.

There are a number of issues remaining in Aristotle's *Nicomachean Ethics* that deserve further study. Book 7 includes Aristotle's most explicit discussion of the Socratic view in ethics; Aristotle offers criticisms of the Socratic view while solving many of the puzzles that beset Socrates. Books 8–9 include Aristotle's extensive discussion of friendship and love (*philia*). In all of philosophy, these books stand as one of the most thorough and insightful investigations of the nature and value of friendship. Only Plato's dialogues on love, i.e. the *Symposium* and the *Phaedrus*, can compare. Finally, we are also now in a position to pursue Aristotle's thought about the nation or city-state (*polis*) as developed in *Politics*. With an understanding of Aristotle's ethics as developed in this chapter, we are in a position to delve deeper into many aspects of Aristotle's practical philosophy. This is certainly a noble and commendable achievement. We may also have achieved something greater in the course of this chapter: it is my hope that we now have a clear idea of what it means to live well, and how to achieve that for ourselves.

CONCLUSION

We are now at the end of this survey of Aristotle's thought, though in many ways we are just beginning. We have focused on numerous key passages, and now we are in a position to read these passages again and again. Aristotle's works reward rereading. This is what we should expect, given that we believe his works are his lecture notes. One can hear the same lecture over and over, and yet new ideas may stand out on different occasions. A lecture is a fluid medium, and our experience of such a medium is likewise fluid. Aristotle's works are like the finest works of Homer, Shakespeare or Dylan; these works are bottomless. Oral poetry, drama and songs all share this fluidity with the medium of lectures. We can dig further and further into Aristotle's concepts and arguments. We have unearthed some astounding gems in the course of our inquiry. There is still much digging to do.

NOTES

INTRODUCTION

1 Alighieri, D. *La Divina Commedia* (edited and annotated by C.H. Grandgent). San Francisco: D.C. Heath & Co., 1933, p. 44.
2 Jeffers, R. *Selected Poems*. New York: Vintage, 1965, p. 66.
3 The will is found in Diogenes Laertius, *Lives of the Philosophers V*. Paris: Didot, 1878, pp. 11–16.
4 This has been suggested by, among others, Barnes. Barnes, J. *Aristotle*. Oxford: Oxford University Press, 1996, p. 4.

1. SCIENCE (*EPISTEME*)

1 The following discussion draws on *Metaphysics Epsilon (6)*, Chapter 1 (1025b1 ff.). The books of the *Metaphysics* are referred to either by number or by the corresponding letter of the Greek alphabet. Barnes, J., ed. *The Complete Works of Aristotle*. Princeton: Princeton University Press, 1984.
2 The pursuit of theoretical knowledge constitutes the best kind of life for a human being. This point will be developed further in Chapter 5 on Aristotle's ethics.
3 Aristotle seems influenced by the idea of the perfection of a circle and circular movement. The heavenly bodies that are themselves perfect spheres undergo unceasing perfect circular motion.
4 For more on the features of first philosophy, see 'The Science of Being: First Philosophy' in Chapter 2.
5 It should be noted that Aristotle's view about the inseparability of numbers and figures is not the only possible view. Philosophers from Pythagoras and Plato to Frege have maintained the independent existence of mathematical entities. For Aristotle, however, mathematical entities are derivative and dependent.
6 Barnes, J., trans. *Posterior Analytics*. Oxford: Clarendon Aristotle Series, 1975.

7 Plato's theory of the Forms is discussed in greater detail in the section of Chapter 2 entitled 'Being Before Aristotle'.

8 Note that the axioms of first philosophy apply to all other scientific fields. But this is not to say that all other scientific truths can be derived from or reduced to the axioms of first philosophy. Rather, Aristotle's claim is that all other scientific truths must be in accordance with the axioms of first philosophy. Thus there is a unity to Aristotle's conception of scientific knowledge, but there is also an appreciation of the distinctness of different domains of science.

9 In the *Prior Analytics* Aristotle develops and formalizes his account of syllogistic reasoning.

10 In defending the law of non-contradiction in *Metaphysics Gamma (4)*, Aristotle adheres to the view expressed here that the axioms cannot be known demonstratively.

11 Consider Plato's theory of recollection as it is developed in the *Meno* and the *Phaedo*. In these dialogues, Plato argues that the soul already possesses knowledge of the Forms, which for Plato serve as the universal terms in the axioms of science. Before the soul's current embodiment, the soul journeyed through the Platonic heaven of Forms; during this journey, the soul came to know each of the Forms completely. Thus one never actually learns anything new; instead what seems like learning is actually recollection of what one already knows. Cooper, J., ed. *Plato: Complete Works*. Indianapolis: Hackett, 1997.

2. BEING OR SUBSTANCE (*OUSIA*)

1 Kirk, G.S., Raven, J.E. and Schofield, M. *The Presocratic Philosophers*. Second Edition. Cambridge: Cambridge University Press, 1983, p. 89.

2 The theory of the Forms emerges in Plato's Middle Period. Representative dialogues include the *Meno*, *Phaedo* and the *Republic*.

3 Ackrill, J.L., trans. *Aristotle's Categories and De Interpretatione*. Oxford: Clarendon Aristotle Series, 1963.

4 The five books of the *Organon* and the focus of each are here detailed. The *Categories* concerns the subject and predicate terms that form propositions. *De Interpretatione* concerns the nature of these propositions, which are the elements of syllogisms. The form of a logical syllogism is developed in the *Prior Analytics*. The form of a demonstrative syllogism, which is how scientific knowledge should be expressed, is developed in the *Posterior Analytics*. The *Topics* is an examination of dialectical arguments. Finally, the *Sophistici Elenchi* is a handbook of bad arguments and fallacies.

5 Note how persistence through change aligns with the Presocratic quest for the substratum, i.e. that which underlies all change and yet remains the same thing.

6 It should be noted that while Empedocles employed the concepts of natural selection and extinction in his biology, Aristotle rejected selection and extinction in the biological realm.

7 Teleology and Aristotle's arguments for it will be treated in greater detail in 'The Four Causes or Explanations (*aitiai*)' and 'Defence of Teleology' in Chapter 3.

3. NATURE (*PHUSIS*)

1 Hardie, R.P. and Gaye, R.K., trans. 'Physics', in Barnes, J., ed. *The Complete Works of Aristotle, Vol. 2*. Princeton: Princeton University Press, 1984. Reprinted by permission.
2 It is not only living things that have a nature; it is a rock's nature, for example, to move downward if left unimpeded. Thus all natural substances have a nature.
3 See Kirk, G.S., Raven, J.E. and Schofield, M. *The Presocratic Philosophers*. Second Edition. Cambridge: Cambridge University Press, 1983, pp. 241–52.
4 See in this connection Ross, W.D. *Aristotle: A Complete Exposition of his Works and Thought*. Cleveland: Meridian, 1959, pp. 74–75.
5 In Aristotle's view, the father contributes form to the child while the mother contributes matter, e.g. blood and tissue. This flawed biological view perhaps explains why Aristotle considers the father alone as the efficient cause rather than both biological parents.
6 See also Ross, *Aristotle*, p. 75.
7 Aristotle's biology thus seems to lack the concepts of evolution and extinction.

4. SOUL (*PSUCHE*)

1 Smith, J.A., trans. 'On the Soul', in Barnes, J., ed. *The Complete Works of Aristotle, Vol. 1*. Princeton: Princeton University Press, 1984. Reprinted by permission.
2 The intellect cannot, however, think contradictions. There is no intelligible form of a contradiction, and so it cannot be an object of thought.
3 *Republic* 507a, *Aristotle* 509c.
4 See 'The Axioms of the Sciences' in Chapter 1.
5 See 'The Chief and Final Good for Human Beings' in Chapter 5.

5. SUCCESS (*EUDAIMONIA*)

1 For a recent and clear introduction to the conflict between conventional moral theory and virtue theory, see van Hooft, S. *Understanding Virtue Ethics*. Malta: Gutenberg Press, 2006.
2 See 'Division of the Sciences According to Aims and Objects' in Chapter 1.
3 Ross, W.D., trans. Revised by Urmson, J.O. 'Nicomachean Ethics', in Barnes, J., ed. *The Complete Works of Aristotle*, Vol. 2. Princeton: Princeton University Press, 1984. Reprinted by permission.

4 For a lucid and thorough treatment of this issue, see Anagnostopoulos, G. *Aristotle on the Goals and Exactness of Ethics*. Berkeley: University of California Press, 1994.

5 See 'Thought' in Chapter 4.

6 Character (*ethos*) and habit (*ethos*), where in the former the first syllable is lengthened.

7 See in particular the following early Socratic dialogues: *Laches*, *Charmides* and *Protagoras*.

8 This intellectualist conception of the virtues explains why Socrates must deny that *akrasia* or incontinence is possible. Socrates maintains that to know the good is to do the good. Aristotle, however, can admit that sometimes we know what is good and yet still do not do it. This is because the irrational part of the soul refuses to obey reason. Aristotle's most direct challenge to Socratic ethics is developed in the *Nicomachean Ethics* Book 7.

9 See 'Principles of Change' in Chapter 3.

BIBLIOGRAPHY

Ackrill, J.L. *Aristotle the Philosopher*. Oxford: Oxford University Press, 1981.
—— *Aristotle's Ethics*. Warnock, M., ed. London: Humanities Press, 1973.
—— ed. *A New Aristotle Reader*. Princeton: Princeton University Press, 1987.
Alexander of Aphrodisias. *In Aristotelis Metaphysica Commentaria*. Hayduck, M., ed. Berlin: G. Reimer, 1891.
Allan, D.J. *The Philosophy of Aristotle*. Second Edition. Oxford: Oxford University Press, 1970.
Anagnostopoulos, G. *Aristotle on the Goals and Exactness of Ethics*. Berkeley: University of California Press, 1994.
Annas, J. *An Introduction to Plato's Republic*. Oxford: Oxford University Press, 1981.
Barnes, J. *Aristotle*. Oxford: Oxford University Press, 1996.
—— 'Aristotle's Theory of Demonstration', *Phronesis* 14, 1969.
—— ed. *The Cambridge Companion to Aristotle*. Cambridge: Cambridge University Press, 1995.
—— ed. *The Complete Works of Aristotle, Vols 1–2*. Princeton: Princeton University Press, 1984.
—— *Early Greek Philosophy*. England: Penguin, 1987.
—— *The Presocratic Philosophers*. New York: Routledge, 1982.
Berti, E., ed. *Aristotle on Science: the Posterior Analytics*. Padua: Editrice Antenore, 1981.
Cooper, J.M., ed. *Plato: Complete Works*. Indianapolis: Hackett, 1997.
—— *Reason and Human Good in Aristotle*. Indianapolis: Hackett, 1986.
Falcon, A. *Aristotle and the Science of Nature*. Cambridge: Cambridge University Press, 2005.
Gill, M.L. *Aristotle on Substance*. Princeton: Princeton University Press, 1989.
Guthrie, W.K.C. *A History of Greek Philosophy*, Vol. VI (Aristotle). Cambridge: Cambridge University Press, 1981.
Hutchinson, D.S. *The Virtues of Aristotle*. London: Routledge and Kegan Paul, 1986.

Irwin, T. and Fine, G., eds. *Aristotle: Selections*. Indianapolis: Hackett, 1995.

Johnson, M.R. *Aristotle on Teleology*. Oxford: Oxford University Press, 2005.

Jones, B. 'An Introduction to the first five chapters of Aristotle's *Categories*'. *Phronesis* 20, 1975.

Kahn, C. *The Verb 'Be' in Ancient Greek*. Reprint Edition. Indianapolis: Hackett, 2003.

Kenny, A. *The Aristotelian Ethics*. Oxford: Oxford University Press, 1978.

—— *Aristotle on the Perfect Life*. Oxford: Oxford University Press, 1992.

Kirk, G.S., Raven, J.E. and Schofield, M. *The Presocratic Philosophers*. Second Edition. Cambridge: Cambridge University Press, 1983.

Kraut, R., ed. *The Cambridge Companion to Plato*. Cambridge: Cambridge University Press, 1992.

Laertius, Diogenes. *Lives of the Philosophers V*. Paris: Didot, 1878.

Lear, J. *Aristotle: The Desire to Understand*. Cambridge: Cambridge University Press, 1988.

Lloyd, G.E.R. *Aristotle: The Growth and Structure of his Thought*. Cambridge: Cambridge University Press, 1968.

—— *Early Greek Science: Thales to Aristotle*. New York: W.W. Norton, 1970.

Long, A.A., ed. *The Cambridge Companion to Early Greek Philosophy*. New York: Cambridge University Press, 1999.

Lewis, F.A. *Substance and Predication in Aristotle*. Cambridge: Cambridge University Press, 1991.

McKeon, R., ed. *The Basic Works of Aristotle*. New York: Modern Library, 2001.

Moravcsik, J.M.E., ed. *Aristotle: A Collection of Critical Essays*. New York: Anchor, 1967.

Nussbaum, M. *The Fragility of Goodness*. Cambridge: Cambridge University Press, 1986.

Pakaluk, M. *Aristotle's Nicomachean Ethics: An Introduction*. Cambridge: Cambridge University Press, 2001.

Rorty, A.O., ed. *Essays on Aristotle's Ethics*. Los Angeles: University of California Press, 1980.

Ross, W.D. *Aristotle: A Complete Exposition of his Works and Thought*. Cleveland: Meridian, 1959.

Sherman, N., ed. *Aristotle's Ethics: Critical Essays*. New York: Rowman & Littlefield, 1999.

van Hooft, S. *Understanding Virtue Ethics*. Malta: Gutenberg Press, 2006.

Witt, C. *Substance and Essence in Aristotle*. Ithaca: Cornell University Press, 1989.

INDEX